MOVEMENTS AND MESSAGES

For Sean

MOVEMENTS AND MESSAGES

Media and Radical Politics in Quebec

by Marc Raboy

translated by David Homel

between the lines

© Between The Lines 1984

Published by:	Between The Lines 427 Bloor Street West Toronto, Ontario, M5S 1X7
Typeset by:	Dumont Press Graphix 97 Victoria Street North Kitchener, Ontario, Canada
Designed by: *Cover designed by:* *Cover photo:*	Dumont Press Graphix Bruce Ernest Andor Journal de Montréal
Printed by:	Les Éditions Marquis Ltée

Originally published in 1983 as *Libérer La Communication: Médias et mouvements sociaux au Québec (1960-1980)*, by Éditions Nouvelle Optique.

Between The Lines is a joint project of Dumont Press Graphix, Kitchener, and the Development Education Centre, Toronto. BTL receives financial assistance from the Ontario Arts Council and Canada Council.

Canadian Cataloguing in Publication Data

Raboy, Marc, 1949-
Movements and Messages

Issued also in French as: Libérer la communication.
ISBN 0-919946-40-2 (bound). -ISBN 0-919946-41-0 (pbk.)

1. Mass media - Political aspects - Quebec (Province).
2. Mass media - Social aspects - Quebec (Province).
3. Social movements - Quebec (Province). I. Title.

HN110.Z9M3 1984   302.2'34'09714   C84-098032-9

TABLE OF CONTENTS

PREFACE TO THE ENGLISH EDITION

Three years ago, when I sat down to write the original version of this work, the first words that came to mind were these: "In Quebec, this is a time for reckoning. . . ." The 1980s were just beginning, and the start of a new decade is as good an excuse as any for political stock-taking.

Those opening words are still valid today, and that is now cause for concern. Not only in Quebec but in English Canada and, indeed, most of the western countries, the left has not yet made the leap from the seventies to the eighties, making its necessary peace with itself and adjusting its strategies and practices to a new context. Understanding where we've come from is still, it seems to me, an essential prerequisite to knowing where we're going.

This book deals with Quebec, of course, but I think it would be wrong to treat it as a "regional study" of interest primarily to specialists. There are certain conclusions to be drawn from the Quebec experience described in the following pages, conclusions pertinent to anyone interested in social and political change, at least in western countries.

There is surely no need by now to emphasize the fact that Quebec is sociologically and culturally "different" from the rest of Canada. If nothing else, the events of the last two decades have caused the cry of difference to be heard, thanks to Quebec's unique responses to the worldwide social upheavals of the 1960s. For the past twenty years, people in English Canada and other parts of the world have been inspired and stimulated by the courageous struggles for national liberation, economic justice and social equality waged by *Québécois* nationalists, union militants and community activists. I would say there has at times been a tendency to romanticize some of this, but there is no doubt that by North American standards, Quebec has been one of the most interesting arenas of social and political activity.

Maybe this is because Quebec had so far to come. This French-speaking corner of North America often seemed to be coasting sleepily through the decades of the thirties, forties and fifties while others were experiencing wrenching changes. The age-old tacit alliance of the Roman Catholic clergy and the Anglo business élite had given way in the mid-1930s to the most powerful — and most conservative — political machine Quebec had ever known: the Union nationale party of Maurice Duplessis. By the time this regime reached its death throes, in the late 1950s, Quebec had reached a stage of marked underdevelopment relative to the rest of the continent.

The "Quiet Revolution" of the early 1960s was thus an accelerated attempt to catch up, in education, industry, social services. The provincial government enjoyed unprecedented popular support, not only from electors, but from social groups as well, as both nationalists and socialists came to see the Quebec State as a vehicle of liberation. Before too long, however, the limits of this approach became apparent and proponents of social change began inventing other forms of political intervention.

Some fifteen years later, history seemed to be repeating itself, with the arrival in power of the pro-sovereignty Parti québécois, and its incapacity to deliver on promises of political independence and social democracy. The failure of the PQ's constitutional strategy and its sledgehammer approach to public sector labour relations recall the dying days of the Quiet Revolution Liberals. The recent return to grace of the fallen Liberal leader Robert Bourassa recalls the resurrection of the Union nationale under Daniel Johnson nearly twenty years earlier. The political stage seems set for a conservative revival; will it also mean a renewal of radical opposition?

Culturally and socially, Quebec is a reflective and introspective society, where artists and intellectuals are placed on a pedestal and ordinary people make ways to speak out about their political ideas. The consciousness of difference in Quebec is by its very existence a subversive threat to the cohesiveness of the Canadian political system, which is based on integration and the centralization of power in the hands of the federal government and corporate leaders. Before the rise of the Parti québécois, the national, social and democratic concerns of progressive people in Quebec tended to blend together. I believe this marriage of concerns will return, now that the PQ is in the process of shattering the last remaining illusions of itself as a potentially progressive force.

Movements and Messages deals with one particular aspect of the Quebec experience: the relationship of different types of communications media to the social and political movements of the sixties and seventies. Again, the Quebec experience in this domain is not only interesting in and of itself, but is pertinent to activists elsewhere, who will inevitably face similar types of problems, if they are not facing them already. It is my profound hope that this important and underestimated area of intervention will occupy a more *coherent* place on the agendas of activists in the 1980s than it did in the past, and that is the main reason I wrote the book.

I deliberately emphasize the word "coherent". Communication has for too long been dealt with frivolously by activists who would not dare take a similar attitude towards political economy or social theory, towards analysis of the workplace or the role of the State. Activists call press conferences, run off leaflets, denounce the bourgeois media, launch alternative journals, watch TV, work as journalists, talk to their neighbours, buy newspapers, make videos . . . we win some and we lose some, but we don't seem to become any more mature. When it comes to communication, we still rely basically on intuition.

Why do I insist on giving the communication question major status? Consider the following contradictory details. In the

United States, the few alternative media that survived the 1960s have become lucrative commercial enterprises. The liberal mainstream press and network television have, since the 1970s, made millions by muckraking the issues first raised by new left groups long since disappeared. In France, the radical newssheet *Libération,* born in the wake of May '68, is now a successful and growing daily — but only after a structural transformation doing away with self-management and equal pay for all workers, giving absolute powers to its editor-in-chief and bringing in a differential pay scale. Meanwhile, all over Europe, people set up their own illegal radio and television transmitters when they can't get satisfaction through official channels.

In Poland, Afghanistan, Nicaragua, El Salvador and Iran, in native communities up and down the Americas, wherever there are cultural minorities and political resistance movements, people infiltrate the communications spectrum by any means possible, as a necessary and essential aspect of their political activity. At the other end of the social scale, wherever there are vested interests in preserving injustice and inequality, we see elaborate plans to control communication. In international forums, the United States stands alone in insisting on all power to the multinational communication empires. In the Soviet Union a photocopy machine is a subversive weapon. The Trilateral Commission states publicly that the main problem in the world is too much democracy, and suggests that a good starting point for a crackdown would be the media.

Indeed, it can be tempting to look the other way. Otherwise, we would have to think about inventing communication strategies for dealing comprehensively with "political" issues like disarmament, or "cultural" issues like relations between the sexes. In Canada, we would have to look critically at the state of the newspaper industry, and broadcasting policy, and the plans to wire us all up for video overkill. And we would still need local and neighbourhood tabloids to keep our chins up as we work for more democratic days ahead.

Quebec is certainly no further ahead than any place else in dealing with these questions, but it has a rich historical experience well worth considering. It may be foolhardy to predict the shape of Quebec politics in the coming years, but I think it is safe to assume that the relationship of communications media to social and political movements will continue to be a key factor. What we have traditionally meant by media is changing, more rapidly and more profoundly than we sometimes care to think — and needless to say, so are movements. There is a need to be supple and ready to adapt to the most subtle changes in the political environment, and this may be the most important thing to keep in mind, for people interested in Quebec, in communication, and, of course, in both.

A personal note. Although English is my mother tongue, I originally wrote the book in French, partly as a gesture of solidarity, partly as an exercise in self-discipline (!), and mostly because it was addressed to people in Quebec engaged in rethinking the sixties and seventies with a view towards the alternative politics of the eighties and nineties. For this edition, some minor changes were made to make the text more accessible to audiences outside Quebec. I hope the reader of this edition will keep in mind that the original version was intended to take its place in a particular universe of discourse, and that translating the words is not enough to transfer the cultural context.

M.R., Montreal,
Autumn, 1983.

ACKNOWLEDGEMENTS

Any work grows out of its author's personal experience. In this case, I have been living with the questions raised in this book for the last fifteen years. I have worked as a professional journalist myself in a variety of media, from the most conventional to the most marginal, and I have been active in community and political organizations.

In order to ask the right questions and begin answering them, I needed to take some critical distance. In a university setting, I was fortunate to find two people willing to help patiently in this process: Professors Yvan Lamonde of McGill University's French Canada Studies Centre and Gertrude J. Robinson of McGill's Graduate Communication Program.

For the original version, Véronique Dassas and Louis Fournier revised and corrected the manuscript. Later, David Homel translated the text into English and Robert Clarke of Between The Lines whipped it into shape.

All along the way, I was the happy recipient of a special kind of family warmth from my two fellow-travellers in daily life, Sheilagh and Paul.

But this work would have had no meaning without the dozens of people in Quebec who are working, sometimes in the shadows with little recognition, to interpret the world in ways that can lead to its transformation. I have had the pleasure of knowing some of these people, and I thank them all.

M.R.

FOREWORD

In Quebec this is a time for reckoning. After twenty years of political, social and cultural agitation, punctuated by alternate periods of repression and programs for co-optation; after the rise and apparent peak of a national liberation movement; after the institutionalization of social conflict by a liberal State which takes more with one hand than it gives with the other; after the disfiguring of the hope and promise of the opposition movements by a retreat into classical political dogmas. . . . After all this and more, it's a time for reckoning.

This study aims to contribute to the growing social literature on the 1960s and 1970s in Quebec by examining the role and impact of *alternative communication practices* in the Quebec context. I have done this by reviewing the social history of the period in such a way as to isolate and evaluate the major attempts at using communications for radical social change, both within and without the mainstream media.

The period was characterized by several types of experience that deserve a special look. For example, the major social opposition movements developed a critique of the mainstream media and tried to launch their own "alternative" means of communication. During the most wrenching moments of crisis — following the political kidnappings of October 1970 and, later, during the general strike of public sector workers in May 1972 — activists attempted to seize direct control of mainstream communication channels. At other times, nascent opposition groups tried to fit themselves out with their own means of political expression, in some cases by manufacturing propaganda, in others through a more traditional usage of existing mass media. And then, within the mainstream media themselves, major conflicts occurred that not only bore out the contradictions and inherent ambiguities of these institutions, but also played a decisive role in social upheaval.

I have essentially directed my attention to the points where opposition movements and means of communication intersected — whether those means were traditional or new. The result is a work of synthesis, based on both available documentation and general socio-historic interpretations of the times, and shaped by my own personal experience and concerns. I believe that the book comes at a time when people in Quebec, as elsewhere, are beginning to ask new questions about the different forms to be taken by militant action. At the same time, in the early 1980s, we are seeing a second generation of alternative press experiences, and an unprecedented crisis in the mass media industries, while important technological changes are paving the way for as yet unimagined transformations in the social patterns of media production and consumption.

In defining my object of analysis as "alternative communication practices", I quickly discovered that communication does not constitute a closed system, but rather is a vaguely-contoured, interactive process with social, political and cultural aspects. The vastness of the field led to a certain arbitrary approach in my selection of material to be covered.

Although they do not make up a homogeneous group, the communication experiences I have considered are also not a disparate series of events. Rather, they are examples that serve to illustrate one basic premise: that communication is an area of ideological and social conflict which demands special attention from groups and individuals trying to resist the patterns of domination prevalent in the cultural, economic, political and social mainstream of our society.

I have paid special attention to the movements that emerged in the early 1960s: to the national struggle of the *Québécois*, to the union movement and to the community efforts known in

Quebec as *le mouvement populaire,* or "popular movement". I
have only touched in passing on other movements just as important, such as the women's and students' movements, the
ecological/environment movement and the efforts of youth
counter-culture groupings. As well, I have not covered regional
experiences or the stories of cultural-linguistic minorities in
Montreal, although several of these could have justifiably been
included.*

Many times I have distinguished between those actions
opposed to the social system per se and those that set out to
reform it. In the course of this I have been able to point out
practices that simply served to reproduce the pattern of domination that was supposedly being opposed, practices that made
their claim in a rhetoric of liberation. My main concern is to
highlight those aspects of each experience that enabled it to resist
being absorbed into mainstream society or stopped it from falling
into its own brand of authoritarianism. The study is theoretically
influenced by the Marxist analysis of the role of mass media in
capitalist society, but I am fully aware of the limitations of this
analysis for understanding cultural phenomena; and especially of
the major strategic problems it can lead to. My critical horizons
are actually somewhat broader, and readers will, I hope, soon
realize my bias in favour of those actors and experiences which
seek to break away not only from the mainstream of capitalist
society but also from all forms of authoritarian social organization. In other words, my bias supports those movements that seek
to break with domination as well as exploitation.

I hope my historical perspective will shed new light on
Quebec's "Quiet Revolution" and the years that followed it.
This period was rich with innovations in communications, new
practices, new awareness, all of which have never been thor-
oughly examined. My study is essentially chronological, not that
I believe that life is a continuum with a determined order of
things, but because it is useful to look at the influence one
experience may have on the following one — especially because

* There is more on the rationale for these omissions in Appendix I: Conscious
Omissions.

we are often dealing here with the personal evolution of individual people. It is pertinent to know, for example, that the critical review *Parti pris* had been in existence for a year when trouble broke out at the major daily *La Presse* in 1964. Or that the launching of the radical newsweekly *Québec-Presse* in 1969 came a year after union leader Marcel Pépin's speech calling for a "Second Front". Or that the attempt to create a left-wing information network, l'Agence de presse libre du Québec, came after the October Crisis of 1970 but before the general strike in the public sector of May 1972.

My study is designed to help identify certain constants, which I hope will lead to a better understanding of the problems of communication in a context of radical social action. Sociological studies abound on the opposition movements that came into being in the west in the 1960s. There are also a great number of theoretical and empirical essays on mass communications in our type of society. But the studies that inquire into the link between the two are rare. In Quebec, no such study exists, and this is a necessary gap to fill for a society in self-reflection.

My study postulates that an accurate reading of the past is necessary if we are to take command of our future. I start from the position that communication practices are part of an ideological domain of conflict in which opposition social movements must make themselves felt. Each of the imperfect attempts looked at in this book can be seen as a step towards a communication strategy grounded in the search for an anti-authoritarian form of socialism. If there can be such a thing as a model to guide future efforts in this direction, it may spring from this kind of synthesis, as well as from the ongoing debates such studies inevitably start. The ultimate purpose of this type of research and reflection is to understand what is at stake in the area of communication and put this understanding to use for our individual and collective liberation.

A GUIDE TO ABBREVIATIONS

APLQ   Agence de presse libre du Québec (Quebec Free Press Agency)

BAEQ   Bureau d'aménagement de l'est du Québec (Eastern Quebec Development Bureau)

CACO   Centre d'animation et de culture ouvrière (Workers' Cultural Action Centre)

CAP   Comité d'action politique (Political Action Committee)

CCRPS   Centre coopératif de recherche en politique sociale (Co-operative Centre for Social Policy Research)

CEQ   Centrale de l'enseignement du Québec (Quebec Teachers' Union)

CFP   Centre de formation populaire (Popular Education Centre)

CIP   Comité d'information politique (Political Information Committee)

CLSC   Centre(s) local des services communautaires (Local Community Services Centre[s])

CRIQ   Centre de recherche et d'information sur le Québec (Centre for Research and Information on Quebec)

CSD   Centrale des syndicats démocratiques (Organization of Democratic Unions)

CSN   Confédération des syndicats nationaux (Confederation of National Trade Unions)

CTCC   Confédération des travailleurs catholiques du Canada (Confederation of Catholic Workers of Canada)

FLP   Front de libération populaire (Popular Liberation Front)

FLQ	Front de libération du Québec (Quebec Liberation Front)
FNC	Fédération nationale des communications (National Communications Federation)
FPJQ	Fédération professionnelle des journalistes du Québec (Federation of Professional Journalists of Quebec)
FRAP	Front d'action politique (Political Action Front)
FTQ	Fédération des travailleurs du Québec (Quebec Federation of Labour)
ICEA	Institut canadien d'éducation des adultes (Canadian Institute for Adult Education)
M-L	Marxist-Leninist(s)
MLP	Mouvement de libération populaire (Popular Liberation Movement)
PQ	Parti québécois
RIN	Rassemblement pour l'indépendance nationale (National Independence Movement)

Translator's note

The English equivalents given in parentheses for these Quebec-based organizations are not official translations adopted by these groups. They are given for easier identification of the groups only. Groups with recognized English-language names are identified only by their English version. For example: the *Rassemblement des citoyens et citoyennes de Montréal,* the RCM, is also known as the Montreal Citizens' Movement, the MCM, and is called the MCM throughout the text.

MEDIA AND SOCIAL CHANGE IN QUEBEC: AN OVERVIEW

Any attempt to impose dates on social processes is in itself arbitrary and contains obvious risks. All the same, observers of Quebec's recent social history easily agree on the capital importance of the year 1960. That year, marked by a change of provincial government, has come to be considered as the beginning of a new era called the "Quiet Revolution".*

However, in analyzing social change, we should not adopt a hard and fast attitude towards this date, as certain writers have pointed out. The editor of *Le Devoir,* Jean-Louis Roy, for one, believes that the basis for change was established in the preceding period, between 1945 and 1960, when a "new social knowledge" came into being. That new knowledge, Roy says, set the stage for radical questioning of the foundations of traditional Quebec society.[1] According to him, a critique of traditional society developed during this period, a critique later passed on to the social body as a whole.

What is of special interest is the importance Roy attaches to the role of communications in this process: "New magazines were created. Their very titles demonstrated the breakthrough that was occurring: *Cité Libre* (1950), *Liberté* (1959), *La Revue socialiste* (1959)." Quebec experienced a "quantitative explo-

* Appendix II contains a chronology of events related to politics and communications in Quebec, 1960-1980.

sion" of information in both the regional and national press at the time. Radio and the new medium of television were enthusiastically welcomed by the *Québécois,* and "Using these powerful new tools of communication, between 1945 and 1960 numerous social groups proposed projects for renewal and modernization to the community."[2]

In other words, communication media played a key role in establishing a "modern" society — that is, an advanced capitalist one — in Quebec. The media demonstrated a capacity to support and promote this new type of society. It was only later that people began to realize that along the way they had sacrificed alternative possibilities.

Analyzing Quebec society from the point of view of political generations, sociologist Serge Proulx has come to the conclusion that the changes soon after 1960 maintained a continuity with traditional society, and were not a total break of the kind that would be called for by the new movements that emerged later.[3] For Proulx the Quiet Revolution was "a time of illusions, of the catch-up generation", during which Quebec tried to get in step with a kind of made-in-U.S.A. modernity, striving to co-opt the values of liberal democracy that Maurice Duplessis' conservative government had placed on the back burner. The ideology incarnated in Duplessis' personality had already begun to erode by the end of the 1940s with events such as the publication of the *Refus global* (Total Rejection) manifesto by a group of artists (1948), the Asbestos strike (1949) and the intellectual protests of the magazine *Cité Libre*.

According to political scientist Roch Denis, who has analyzed community and worker protests of this period, the union movement in particular experienced a renaissance during the 1950s, with grassroots protests aimed at Quebec's leading institutions.[4] Two examples of this shift — and by no means the least important — were the producers' strike at Radio-Canada (1959), and the journalists' walk-out at *La Presse* (1958).* Both of these labour conflicts strengthened ties between manual and intellectual workers.[5]

* The *La Presse* walk-out is discussed in chapter 2.1.

By 1959, then, at both the summit and the base of Quebec society, everyone agreed it was time for change. Conditions were ripe for social reform, although questions of class conflict remained in the background, at least at the start.[6]

1. Catching up: the rise of the protest generation

In 1960, after the death of Duplessis, after the aborted reform movement of his successors Paul Sauvé and Antonio Barrette and the subsequent election of Jean Lesage's new Liberal regime, the mainstream of society moved from a "respect for traditions" to take up the "challenge of progress". Denis Monière, the author of a sweeping history of ideologies in Quebec, sees this as a turning point in Quebec's ideological development, signalling the beginning of a new era.[7] The early sixties were characterized by a certain harmony, but new forms of social action were soon to appear and would challenge society in a much more basic way.

Serious opposition to the consensus of the Quiet Revolution arose in 1963, and it is easy to understand why when we take into account the evaluation of the period made by sociologist Dorval Brunelle.[8] In Brunelle's view, the so-called "revolution" was really nothing more than a "reorganization of alliances within the bourgeoisie", designed to strengthen the ties between financial and industrial capital and to smooth the transition to State monopoly capitalism. The main characteristic of the time was an insistence on the need to use the Quebec State as the main moving force, taking charge of collective aspirations.

As disillusionment settled in, a new actor entered the scene: the "protest generation", as Serge Proulx calls it. New social movements appeared, such as the citizens' committees that began to flower in urban inner-city neighbourhoods; the movement for national independence crystallized; intellectuals turned toward socialist ideas. In general, as Proulx says, protest was characterized by an "interpenetration of the nationalist movement and the social and socialist demands made by other movements."[9] And, in the emergence of this protest movement many writers accord great importance to the little intellectual and political magazines of the time, especially *Parti pris,* about which we will say more later.

In his book *The Canadian Left,* an historical study of left-wing currents in Canada, Norman Penner sees *Parti pris* as the incarnation of the protest movement in Quebec in the early 1960s.[10] According to Denis Monière, the ideological break-throughs and expressions of the contradictions of the modernization process, first stated in the little magazines of which *Parti pris* was the most important, were the key factors in the emergence of a Quebec socialist movement.[11] Finally, says Roch Denis: "Within the Quiet Revolution, as a series of social and democratic issues demanded resolution, a group of intellectuals attempted to settle — at least on a theoretical level — the left-over questions that had never been solved in Quebec."[12]

Labour unions had played a significant role in focusing protest against the Duplessis regime. But after 1960, feeling they had already gained some power for themselves, unions joined the social consensus that took shape in support of the new Liberal regime in Quebec. Labour sociologist Hélène David considers this period to be nothing but an interregnum. She points out that several of the reforms about to become law had been the object of union demands for some years.[13] Besides, the new regime needed the support of the union centrals if it wanted to forestall working-class opposition to its power, before that opposition could be turned into an organized force.

With the reform of the labour relations system in 1964 and the massive unionization of the public sector that followed, a new source of potential opposition to established power came into being. In 1960 the CSN (Confédération des syndicats nationaux, or Confederation of National Trade Unions) had been created after the secularization of the old Confédération des travailleurs catholiques du Canada. Now, unionized workers, most of them with the CSN or in the educational system, began to push an impressive list of demands on issues that had long been trampled underfoot by the old regime. Though the national question dominated social conflict under the Liberals, it was the worker unrest in hospitals, schools and other sectors that helped prepare the ground for the Liberals' defeat in 1966.[14]

Only at the beginning of the 1970s would the union movement, led by the CSN, come to an ideological parting of ways with the socio-economic system of State monopoly capitalism. In the critical analyses of the earlier period, however, a single union conflict is most often cited as the definitive end of the Quiet Revolution. And what's more, the union dispute was in the communication sector: at the Montreal daily *La Presse,* the most important mass-media enterprise in the private sector in Quebec.

Hélène David writes that during this clash, which lasted through 1964 and 1965, "It became only too clear that there were strong links between the board of directors of the largest newspaper organization in Quebec and the Liberal Party."[15] And according to Dorval Brunelle, "Beyond this conflict, whose real source was information policy, the rights of Quebec employers were at stake."[16]

The battle between the owners of *La Presse* and their journalists was above all centred on the politics of information (see chapter 2.1). Like subsequent struggles at the paper and elsewhere in the media, it was to demonstrate the important relationship between internal institutional struggles and the external pattern of social evolution in Quebec.

By 1965 and 1966, the idea of a Quiet Revolution orchestrated from above became more and more open to question. At the same time, a large-scale grassroots movement sprung up, accompanied by a groundswell later known as *le mouvement populaire.*

Several writers contend that 1963 really marked the beginnings of this movement.[17] During that year, a new approach emerged within the traditional social service organizations working among the "underprivileged" in Montreal, an approach based on the ideology of participation and a strategy of community organizing. According to authors Charles Côté and Yannik Harnois, this practice, known as *animation sociale,* responded to "a need to restructure communication", a need brought on by the new sociological and technical changes taking place alongside

the modernization of Quebec society.[18] Social animation as practised by the Conseil des Oeuvres de Montréal, an important
Catholic charity, attempted to "teach people how to communicate better and work in groups more efficiently."[19] In fact,
the more this kind of practice evolved, the more it moved
towards radical social change, towards a self-directing, participatory society — at least in its declared intentions.

The climate of the Quiet Revolution favoured the development of this type of community organizing. During the early
years, emphasis was placed on the actions of small groups and on
the articulation of particular demands in issues such as housing
and the use of community resources. Frédéric Lesemann and
Michel Thiénot of the University of Montreal's School of Social
Work have indicated how the Quebec State used some of the
techniques and even the language of community organizing for
its own ends, in cases where official institutions got involved for
their own purposes. Beginning in 1963, the Bureau d'aménagement de l'est du Québec (BAEQ — Eastern Quebec Development
Bureau) used community organizing techniques and the principle
of participation in regional planning.[20] A few years later, this
kind of organizing was consciously tied in with a systematic
utilization of the mass media in a large-scale program of public
education through community television known as TEVEC
(*Télévision communautaire*).[21]

After 1965, however, a second generation of more critical
popular groups emerged, influenced by an embryonic socialist
ideology and setting themselves against established power.
These groups adopted the notion of "popular power" as an alternative focus. The author of the first full-scale study of the popular groups of the 1960s, Donald McGraw, deems this generation
to be transitional, in the sense that, although the groups went
beyond the tendencies of their predecessors to work within the
system, they had not yet severed all ties with the mainstream.
That would happen a few years later, and would involve a
breakaway from both dominant society and the rest of the
Quebec left.[22]

These transitional groups slowly became stronger, and went

on to become part of the larger social movement. An example that illustrates McGraw's point was the 1967 launching, in the Saint-Henri quarter of Montreal, of the first neighbourhood newspaper to be founded by a group of citizens: *L'Opinion ouvrière* (Workers' Views). That paper was soon overtaken from the left by a much more politicized competitor, *Le Pouvoir ouvrier* (Workers' Power). This was probably the first example of the "passing on the left" that was to become of the characteristics of Quebec social movements in the 1970s.[23]

The years between 1967 and 1969 were marked by progressive radicalization on all fronts. These were years of upheaval in all western countries, but the situation in Quebec gave rise to some very particular phenomena. The period was full of new initiatives in communications based directly on the social movements of the time. Two articles that appeared in 1971 are instrumental to an understanding of the specific role of communications in those years. The articles were published in Quebec under the signature "B.R., journalist" in order to protect the identity of the author who was then employed in the Montreal mass media.[24]

Writing shortly after the October Crisis of 1970, "B.R." asked: What attitude should be taken towards the mass media that provide us with information? Analyzing the development of the capitalist press in Quebec, with its economic concentration, its enthusiastic conservatism and its stand against union militancy, this covert journalist concluded that what people needed was *counter-information*. However, attempts in that direction at the time — the writer was mainly referring to the weekly *Québec-Presse* and the FLQ's policy of direct action — raised more questions than they solved.

2. The drift to polarized politics

The events of the late 1960s caused a clear-cut radicalization among participants in popular movements. According to Donald McGraw, in a society faced with the erosion of ideals of democratic participation and with increased State repression, various strains of Marxist analysis became more attractive, both as philosophic thought and strategic guide.[25] In addition, by 1971 the union movement had radically changed its attitude towards the political system. As in 1964, a union conflict at the daily *La Presse* was the catalyst for an important change in class relations; this time the conflict set into motion the inter-union Common Front of 1972. After 1972, the demands of the union and popular movements would become increasingly anchored in Marxist thought and in a nascent political strategy whose main principle was the creation of "the Party". The promoters of this strategy gave great importance to propaganda, or ideological struggle.[26] Serge Proulx writes:

> By efficiently infiltrating the union apparatus, Marxist militants were able to politicize Quebec unions. And through the media, they were also able to communicate the image of the Employer-State, against which the working class must struggle by any means necessary.[27]

In 1980, four authors — Marielle Désy, Yves Vaillancourt, Marc Ferland and Benoît Lévesque — together prepared a provisional analysis of the militant experience of the time and pointed out the gap between theory and practice in the work of left-wing militants.[28] The result of the gap, they concluded, was that progressive currents had been isolated and efficiency lessened.[29] According to these writers, the problem was that left-wing words were thought to equal left-wing action. Activists had presumed that the sought-after base would automatically rally around whatever movement had the correct political line. This turned out not to be the case: On the contrary, much of the agitation of the 1970s ended up weakening the left in several areas, as we shall see (chapter 4). In fact we are only now beginning to understand the experience of those years.

The polar opposite to the activities of the supporters of the "revolutionary party" was a series of official social service reforms in the early 1970s. "Social animation" disappeared once and for all as the role of the community organizer became institutionalized, first with the federal LIP (Local Initiative Projects) and OFY (Opportunities for Youth) grant programs and later with new organs of social integration implemented by Quebec, such as the Centres locaux de services communautaires (CLSC — Local Community Services Centres).[30] In this way the State took over community organizing: The ranks of the CLSCs were filled by ex-militants from oppositional groups who woke up one morning to find themselves para-public employees earning civil-servant salaries and enjoying all the benefits of full-time permanent employment without ever having to answer to their original constituencies.

This development caused a major realignment within the popular movement, but politically-committed militants went on working among autonomous community groups. For the far left, these groups became the place for making contact with the masses. In a way, this type of action continued the tradition of left-wing groups and political parties from before 1960, back when a militant serving in a popular front was supposed to take a stand according to the strategy established by the political group to which he or she belonged.[31]

Despite this polarization, some activists tried to carve themselves a place between these two extremes. Many new groups arose out of urban, ecological or feminist movements,[32] each one bringing along its own communication strategy — without necessarily learning from its predecessors. The political changes that brought the Parti québécois to power in 1976 exacerbated the split between the extreme left and "social democracy", but it soon gave way to these new movements. A brand new series of contradictions created by the PQ echoed the year 1960 and what came after it.

At the same time, the agitated state of the traditional mass media proved once more that this sector could not be ignored in an overall analysis of Quebec society, especially in understanding the connections between social movements and communication. Once again, internal conflicts within the media took a prominent place during a vast series of strikes in 1977 and 1978, as well as in 1980 and 1981, when journalists at Radio-Canada and *Le Devoir* went out. Again it became clear how important a role these creators of information had played since the beginning of the Quiet Revolution. The demystification of the role of communication institutions, the fight for free information against institutional obstacles and the efforts to launch truly alternative media all had to reckon with the new challenge to the social role of communications that came from mainstream media.

3. Mainstream media: conflicts and profits

Under Duplessis, in general, the Quebec press was one of the bastions of ideological harmony and social tranquility. Gérard Pelletier, at the time a journalist and later a federal cabinet minister, tells how labour movement news — to name just one sector of activity — was virtually absent from the media until *Le Devoir* began covering labour conflicts at the end of the 1940s. And when the press could no longer ignore these events, as in the case of the 1949 Asbestos strike, its coverage was rather strange. Pelletier writes:

> The mainstream press is there to "inform", so we're told, but every day its readers are treated to praises of capitalism and free enterprise, and denunciations of communism and socialism. On all fronts, from news stories or editorials, this so-called informational press is carrying out a life-and-death struggle. This press is a militant one. Its so-called neutrality and cherished objectivity did not amount to much when it came to a situation like the Asbestos strike. [33]

Among other things, the Quiet Revolution upset the traditional conservatism of the mass media. With this period, "the most tumultuous time in the history of the Quebec press" began. [34] From 1958 to 1967, every major newspaper in Quebec either changed ownership, administrators, publisher or editor-in-chief. [35] The situation at *La Presse* was only the tip of the iceberg.

The larger newspapers may have been living through a "tumultuous" time, but they were simply following the movement of the society to which they belonged, and in which, along with other institutions, they helped maintain the social consensus. [36] Even when the press allowed itself a more critical and dynamic role, it still remained strictly capitalist, guided by the ideology of its own neutrality regarding social conflicts. This situation inspired the magazine *Parti pris* to comment in the fall of 1964: "The structures of a truly free press remain to be created."[37]

This comment is borne out by a phenomenon like the concentration of ownership in private newspaper enterprises, a tendency that increased dramatically towards the middle of the decade. The first example involved the group that was to become the most powerful: the organization associated with the Franco-Ontarian financier, Paul Desmarais.[38]

In 1964, the Corporation des valeurs Trans-Canada (CVTC — Trans-Canada Corporation Fund) bought up three Montreal weeklies, *Le Petit Journal, Photo-Journal* and *Dernière Heure.* The following year, CVTC was absorbed by Enterprises Gelco Ltée, 75 per cent owned by Paul Desmarais. In 1966, Gesca Ltée, a branch of Gelco, bought *La Presse.* In 1968, Paul Desmarais became the most important share-holder (with 30 per cent) of Power Corporation, a company with a variety of interests and one of the largest in Canada. In Quebec, big capital and the press became intertwined more tightly than ever. And this concentration has since continued without let-up.

Taking advantage of *La Presse*'s absence during the long strike of 1964-65, entrepreneur Pierre Péladeau launched a competing daily called *Journal de Montréal.* Founded on a commercial formula that it has been refining ever since, this tabloid became the flagship of the Québécor publishing empire.

By 1970, a small number of consortia controlled some 50.6 per cent of all French-language daily newspapers published in Quebec.[39] Throughout Canada between 1970 and 1980 corporate concentration increased, with the number of groups decreasing and their market share increasing. In Quebec, simple monopoly seemed to be the rule. Eventually 90 per cent of French-language daily newspapers came to be controlled by three groups: Québécor (46.5 per cent), Gesca (28.8 per cent) and UniMédia (14.7 per cent). There is only one independent French-language paper left in Quebec: *Le Devoir.*[40]

The English-language press, meanwhile, is largely controlled from the outside; only the Sherbrooke *Record* is independent.

TABLE 1

Paul Desmarais' media involvement

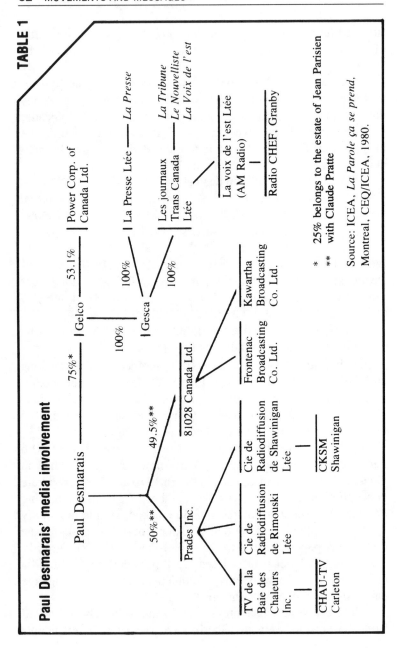

Paul Desmarais —— 75%* —— | Gelco —— 53.1% —— | Power Corp. of Canada Ltd.

|100% | La Presse Ltée —— | La Presse

| Gesca —— 100% —— | Les journaux Trans Canada Ltée —— | La Tribune / Le Nouvelliste / La Voix de l'est

La voix de l'est Ltée (AM Radio)

Radio CHEF, Granby

49.5%** —— | 81028 Canada Ltd. —— Frontenac Broadcasting Co. Ltd. / Kawartha Broadcasting Co. Ltd.

50%** —— | Prades Inc. —— TV de la Baie des Chaleurs Inc. / Cie de Radiodiffusion de Rimouski Ltée / Cie de Radiodiffusion de Shawinigan Ltée

CHAU-TV Carleton

CKSM Shawinigan

*   25% belongs to the estate of Jean Parisien
** with Claude Pratte

Source: ICEA, *La Parole ça se prend*, Montreal, CEQ/ICEA, 1980.

The Montreal daily, *The Gazette*, belongs to the English-Canadian Southam group, whereas *The Montreal Star*, before its closing in 1979, was owned by the Thomson chain. Thomson, the largest owner of newspapers in Canada, has over forty dailies in its stable, including Toronto's prestigious *Globe and Mail* with its pretensions of being English Canada's national newspaper. The closing of two more big dailies — the Winnipeg *Tribune* and the Ottawa *Journal* — in the autumn of 1980 incited the federal government to create a Royal Commission on Newspapers (the Kent Commission). However, Ottawa was in no hurry to follow up on the recommendations of the Commission, especially one that would force the Thomson conglomerate to divest itself of a number of its papers.

In the realm of radio and TV the situation has been somewhat less dramatic, given the "safeguard" represented by State corporations. Yet there has still been a trend towards concentration in private electronic media, which despite their purely commercial vocation have attempted to pass as public service and information vehicles.[41] In this area, Quebec concentration also began in the 1960s, when Raymond Crépeault created the first private radio network in Canada, the Civitas Corporation (Radiomutuel). Since that time, Radiomutuel has grown apace and it boasted a sales figure of close to $30 million in 1980.[42]

The dependence of the media on the business world due to increased concentration is a well-established fact. Even those media that profess political autonomy become dependent on the economic system as soon as they try to penetrate the commercial mass market. The common interests of private enterprise and the State are most evident in the allocation of industry and government advertising budgets. This was well illustrated in Quebec by the experiences of pro-sovereignty papers such as *Québec-Presse* and *Le Jour*, which were systematically discriminated against by those who controlled the spending of public money (see chapters 3.1 and 4.5).[43] In his study of Quebec business, political scientist Pierre Fournier discovered that 32.8 per cent of all businessmen refused to place ads in newspapers opposed to the political system, which goes a long way towards explaining why *Québec-Presse* and *Le Jour* had such difficulty in staying afloat.[44]

The grip of this dependence becomes even more apparent when we consider that, in general, the same social élite owning the big industrial concerns also owns the mass media in Canada, and that concentration is more severe in Quebec than elsewhere in Canada. Power Corporation, for example, is not only one of the largest business complexes in Canada, but is also indirectly the biggest media owner in Quebec.[45]

The effect of this concentration of capital on the media is truly striking. The communications sector is one of the most profitable in Canada. Between 1958 and 1968, profits ranged from 23 to 30 per cent a year after taxes, compared to 18 and 15 per cent respectively for the manufacturing and industrial sectors.[46] The media industry continued to enjoy growing profits in the 1970s: From 1971 to 1976 the eight major Canadian companies in this sector increased their revenues by over 20 per cent a year.[47] In Quebec, the radio station CJMS alone made $2.7 million in profits in 1975, the year before a long, hard labour conflict over union recognition.[48] In 1976, the fourteen Quebec dailies rang up $210 million in gross advertising profits, not counting the $85 million brought in by sales.[49] In the first nine months of 1978, Télé-Métropole (Montreal's Channel 10) turned in record profits of $6.8 million, totally outdistancing its revenues from the preceding year.[50] As for Québécor Inc., it recorded $12 million worth of profits with its Quebec-based publications in 1980.[51]

These figures show just how golden the media's Midas touch remains. Over the last few years there has been a tendency to present corporate concentration as a necessary evil to insure business profitability, when in fact profits have risen steadily. As the Kent Commission points out, profits of Canadian daily papers remain well above returns on capital in most other industries.[52]

The 1970 Senate committee study of Canadian mass media (the Davey Committee) discovered that the Canadian public considered their newspapers to be essential media, although they admitted that television had a greater influence.[53] Ten years

TABLE 2

Major mass media ownership groups in Quebec, 1979

Desmarais Group	Newspapers	*La Presse* (Montreal)
		Le Nouvelliste (Trois-Rivières)
		La Tribune (Sherbrooke)
		La Voix de l'est (Granby)
	Radio/TV	CHEF-Radio (Granby)
		CKSM-Radio (Shawinigan)
		CHAU-TV (Carleton)
Québécor Inc.		*Journal de Montréal*
		Journal de Québec
		8 national weeklies
		10 regional weeklies
UniMédia Inc.		*Le Soleil* (Quebec)
		Le Quotidien (Chicoutimi)
		2 national weeklies
		2 regional weeklies
		7 metropolitan weeklies
Civitas Corp.		5 AM radio stations (*Radiomutuel*)
		1 FM radio station
Beaudem Ltée		7 AM radio stations
		2 FM radio stations
		2 TV stations
Télé-Métropole Inc./ Pathonic Communications		4 TV stations
CFCF Inc.		1 TV station
		1 AM radio station
		1 FM radio station
		1 short-wave radio station

There are also several regional groups. Note that most of the English-language press belongs to Anglo-Canadian groups based outside Quebec. Source: ICEA, *La parole ça se prend*, Montreal, CEQ/ICEA, 1980; *Financial Post*, special report "Inside the Media", September 22, 1979.

later, the Royal Commission on Newspapers found that the majority of Canadians still believed that newspapers were the best suited medium for the "essential" and "comprehensive" information they needed.[54]

A study done for the Quebec government in 1972 showed that *Québécois* feel the same way about their daily press. The SORECOM study paid special attention to dailies, since "From the strict perspective of information, the written press — especially the daily press — occupies a more important role in relation to other means of information".[55] The SORECOM inquiry pointed to the fact that 80 per cent of all people in Quebec read a daily paper; two-thirds of them read a weekly paper. On the other hand, 94 per cent listen to the radio and 97 per cent watch television. Eighty per cent of the population said it wished to hear the day's news; and the main reason respondents gave for using media at all was "to stay informed". However, the SORECOM study did not conclude whether people actually find the information they are looking for in the various media they consume.[56]

The corresponding figures for Canada, cited by Wallace Clement and based on 1972 Statistics Canada data, show that 90 per cent of all Canadians read a newspaper, 95.8 per cent watch television and 97.6 per cent listen to the radio. As Clement comments, "Access to the media seems to be a very high priority for Canadians and access to the media means that the media has access to Canadians as well".[57]

By 1980, the number of Canadian households with at least one television set had climbed to 98 per cent. However, the watchers were more divided: More than 50 per cent of all Canadian homes had TV coverage through cable hookups and 10 per cent owned converters that provided even more channels. The average Canadian spent 191 minutes a day watching television in 1980.[58]

Considering how important the media are to the population as a whole — and considering the danger of conflict of interest between owners of enterprises and owners of the media — the fact that these two groups of owners are becoming one and the same is cause for concern. In Quebec, this trend seems to be particularly pronounced.

Meanwhile, the number of daily papers goes on decreasing, along with print runs, while a realignment is taking place within the market. True, the total number of copies printed rose 12 per cent between 1960 and 1976, but the population increased 18 per cent during that same period. Between 1971 and 1976, there was an absolute decrease in copies of 5 per cent, and in Montreal fewer copies of daily newspapers were printed in 1976 than in 1964.[59] These figures do not even reflect the disappearance of *Montréal-Matin* in 1978 and *The Montreal Star* in 1979.

The state of the weeklies is no more healthy. The "national" weekly is peculiar to Quebec; the SORECOM study counted eight of them, not counting the seventy-five regional informational weeklies and another seventy-five entertainment weeklies. In 1980, some twenty of these weeklies belonged to affiliates of the Québécor group owned by Pierre Péladeau; ten others belonged to UniMédia, the third largest press group in Quebec since its acquisition of Quebec City's *Le Soleil*.[60]

The ownership problem in the press is often seen in strictly economic terms. But corporate concentration has social ramifications as well. The most interesting part of the Kent Commission report contains a qualitative analysis of how the newspaper business is run, concluding that there is a very clear general relationship between the type of ownership and whether the emphasis is placed on public service, or on company profitability.[61] According to this analysis, those papers owned by diversified conglomerates — companies with considerable holdings in enterprises other than newspapers — are on the high end of the profitability scale. In Quebec, the Gesca group is this kind of enterprise. At a mid-point on the scale of service and profits is the enterprise whose interests are limited to communications: The Québécor and UniMédia groups would fall into this category. And down at the public service end of the scale are the independent papers, *Le Devoir*, for example. The Commission even concluded that the newspaper industry seems to be the only one in Canada in which the profit rate is clearly in an inverse proportion to the quality of the product.

The type of ownership also has a bearing on social relations within the media. As "B.R." put it in 1971:

> Entering a large newspaper empire usually destroys militant unionism. Faced with the immense capital resources at the disposal of these empires, a union has to think twice before a showdown, since it has little chance of coming out in one piece.... Concentration creates displacement in power relations, resulting in disproportionate ones.... The phenomenon of concentration does not change the ideology being transmitted, but it does permit greater direct control.[62]

As far back as 1969, the Quebec journalists' association, the Fédération professionnelle des journalistes du Québec, denounced concentration as a threat to freedom of the press.[63] In the FPJQ's opinion, the public's right to honest, complete, high-quality information was severely compromised by the interests of capital. This issue was at the heart of many union conflicts in the information business during the 1970s (see, for instance, Chapter 4.5).

In August 1973, the FPJQ, the Quebec Press Council and the three union centrals* took a stand against Paul Desmarais' intention to buy Quebec City's *Le Soleil*. But the pressure they exerted had only a symbolic effect. It stalled the transaction until January 1974, when *Le Soleil* was purchased by Les Journaux Trans-Canada (UniMédia), a group run by a friend and associate of Desmarais, Jacques Francoeur.[64]

The efforts of a common front to block the launching by Civitas of a third network of commercial television in Quebec were rewarded with greater success. Thanks in part to this opposition, the Civitas group's attempt failed twice, in 1973 and 1975. This common front has since become a permanent working group within the Institut canadien d'éducation des adultes (ICEA), one of Quebec's main adult education organizations. The ICEA's working group has been one of the most important

---

* CSN (Confédération des syndicats nationaux); FTQ (Fédération des travailleurs du Québec); CEQ (Centrale de l'enseignement du Québec).

meeting-places for people interested in future alternative projects in communications.[65]

When we consider the nature of ownership in the private and public sectors, examine the power represented by advertising and look closely at the relationships between media owners, businessmen and politicians, it is obvious that the Quebec mass media are hardly fertile ground for expressing unorthodox ideas. The only exceptions to the rule arise as a result of intense pressure applied by organizations outside the media themselves, or from union and professional organizations of media workers. Though it is no doubt useful to be present in the mainstream media, it is equally important to recognize the limits of those media and thus take the necessary steps towards creating forums of counter-information. In my opinion, any strategy for establishing *free* information must take into account both traditional and new media — and understand the conflicts in both.

2

TOWARDS A PARALLEL PRESS MOVEMENT

The opening years of the Quiet Revolution coincided with what one writer considered to be "the golden age of contemporary Quebec journalism".[1] True, the changes Quebec society was experiencing brought a breath of fresh air into the musty newsrooms of the larger newspapers. The venerable Montreal daily *La Presse* was the most remarkable example of this greening. Its internal changes are a sort of microcosm for what was occurring in society as a whole, and events at the paper were to blow the cover off the social consensus that was typical of the Quiet Revolution.

But even before that, other storm warnings had appeared on the horizon. The policies of the supposedly enlightened governing regime in Quebec began to be heavily criticized, especially by small-circulation magazines, with one in particular, *Parti pris,* leading the way. These magazines did not claim to be in opposition to the mass media per se — that is, they did not see themselves as alternative media — but they did oppose the social system. They worked out a number of interpretations of the social and political reality of the times and took a stand against the dominant ideology transmitted by the official institutions of this newly transformed place called Quebec. In doing so the magazines provided an ideological basis for the opposition movements that were to rise up in the middle of the 1960s.

From 1965 onward — and especially after 1968 — pockets of opposition began to form in virtually all sectors of social activity. Fundamental in this opposition was a newborn awareness of the role of the organs of mass communication in the maintenance of the system being challenged. This awareness was supplemented by the realization that sources of counter-information had to be established: means of communication that would be independent of political and economic authority; media that would defend the cause of workers, common people and Quebec nationalists.

1. La Presse and the end of the Quiet Revolution

As early as 1958, events at *La Presse* hinted at things to come.[2] In October of that year a *La Presse* journalist, Roger Mathieu, was elected president of the Confédération des travailleurs catholiques du Canada, precursor of the Confédération des syndicats nationaux (CSN). But management refused to allow Mathieu a leave of absence to assume the post. The union responded with an illegal strike that would change not only its own members' working conditions but also the face of journalism throughout Quebec.

This strike was both a sign of things to come and an indication of exactly what was at stake within the mass media. As journalist Pierre Godin puts it:

> At *La Presse* in 1958, there was a group of journalists who wanted to throw out medieval authority structures, senseless journalistic practices, who realized it was time to put the paper's form and content in step with reality, and who were against the boss's anti-union streak that threatened to erase recent gains.[3]

At the time, *La Presse* displayed a "benevolent neutrality" towards the Duplessis regime, but one of the results of the 1958 strike was the reorganization of the paper under Jean-Louis Gagnon, a dynamic journalist with close ties to the Liberal Party. "Gagnon's main contribution would be to put his paper in step with the new society that was on its way," writes Pierre Godin.[4]

However, because of a power struggle within the Du Tremblay family, which owned the paper, *La Presse* did not back the

Liberals in the 1960 elections. This was despite the fact that the chairman of the publicity and propaganda commission of the Quebec Liberal Federation, lawyer Claude Ducharme, was one of the strongmen on the paper's board of directors. Furious, and realizing how important *La Presse* was politically, the incoming Liberal Premier Jean Lesage got Ducharme to force Gagnon to leave and to have him replaced by a man who was just as dynamic, Gérard Pelletier.

Sponsored by *La Presse* heiress Angelina Du Tremblay, Gagnon went on to launch *Le Nouveau Journal,* which was to last nine months over 1961 and 1962. Meanwhile Pelletier, one of the founders of *Cité Libre* and ex-editor-in-chief of the CSN's journal *Le Travail,* set up shop at *La Presse*.

Pelletier was to play a somewhat ambiguous role at *La Presse*. Pierre Godin waxes ironically about him: "The destiny of one of these reformist intellectuals seems to have been to provide the established system ways of adapting to new social conditions, thereby keeping it from the edge of destruction."[5] But in the early days of Pelletier's stewardship there did appear to be real change in the wind at the paper. Urged on by its new competitor, *Le Nouveau Journal, La Presse* became a true pioneer in political journalism. For the first time, political coverage began systematically to go beyond the surface of events to analyze their implications. The paper increased its Quebec City staff, better to follow the administrative changes taking place at the governmental level. Journalists enjoyed a free rein such as they had only dreamed about before. The *La Presse* newsroom at this time harboured such independent spirits as Pierre Vallières, Michel van Schendel and Pierre Bourgault, journalists who would soon become involved in some of the most radical projects of the day (respectively, the reviews *Révolution québécoise* and *Socialisme,* and the pro-independence party, the Rassemblement pour l'indépendance nationale (RIN). (See chapter 2.2.)

According to Dorval Brunelle, "As long as there was competition between two large daily papers, journalists enjoyed freedom of expression and a kind of elbow room never before encountered, and they used it to expose and criticize the regime's internal disparities and financial scandals."[6]

But from 1964 onward, positions hardened. Although *La Presse,* as press historians Jean Hamelin and André Beaulieu put it, "was not afraid to display a certain amount of free thinking when it came to financial and political power",[7] this attitude withered once the government put a halt to the reform movement. Political power, always present in the upper levels of *La Presse,* put pressure on the paper's board of directors to halt the wave of criticism. The government began to publicly question the integrity of people working in information. When Gérard Pelletier, to his credit, refused to exercise his right to censor what went into his newspapers, the directors knew they would have to do something drastic. In September 1964, after the paper's typographers went on strike, the directors of *La Presse* decreed a lock-out and closed down the paper.[8] The lock-out lasted seven months and in the public mind during that time — as assessed by Hélène David — the paper's "return to an information policy and an editorial line that did not involve investigation and criticism of governmental policies came to be seen as tantamount to censorship."[9]

The journalists, in their state of forced unemployment, published thirty issues of their own paper, *La P... libre,* with a circulation of fifty-five thousand. They continued criticizing and analyzing, as an ominous atmosphere settled over other papers where traditional journalism laboured on.

La Presse's employees were not the only ones attacked by the government's manoeuvring; according to Dorval Brunelle, anyone in opposition was a target:

> Obviously, as far as the ruling class was concerned, the issue was not just a handful of journalists working in one of its enterprises. Freedom of expression and the right to information — the control of the free flow of ideas, policies and counter-policies — was on the line.[10]

Typical of this new development: In October 1964 journalists received formal orders to keep quiet about the growing separatist movement in at least three dailies, *Le Soleil, L'Événement-Journal* and *L'Action.*[11]

The conflict at *La Presse* soon became a *cause célèbre* on the left. In the newborn magazine *Révolution québécoise*, Jean Rochefort wrote: "*La Presse* is not just a commercial enterprise. It's a public service, since it is both an essential means of information in the democratic process *and* a virtual monopoly, the only big French-language daily paper in the province."[12] The left saw the *La Presse* conflict as a sign of how much Quebec capitalists feared the separatist movement and the socialist ideas it tended to propagate.

At the year's end, after seven months, the conflict was settled to the detriment of the journalists. Shortly after, in March 1965, Gérard Pelletier was fired. He had maintained total silence during the paper's closing, costing him his employees' respect without winning that of his superiors. A chapter in the history of Quebec journalism had ended.

But a more important product of the conflict was the collapse of co-operation between the government and social movements. Economic and political power in Quebec and those who favoured social progress parted ways, and opposition movements began to realize what was at stake within the mainstream media.

2. Parti pris and the new voices of protest

The conflict at *La Presse* signalled the end of the Quiet Revolution. But this "revolution" had seen its share of critics from the start. Indeed, socialist tendencies, very different from those maintained by the Liberal regime, had taken root some time earlier, especially after 1963. One of the favoured means of giving voice to this critical spirit was the small-circulation political review. Several reviews aimed at intellectuals and strongly influenced by radical nationalist ideology were launched at this time.

The first of these little reviews had appeared as far back as 1959. Called *Revue socialiste*, published by the group Action socialiste pour l'indépendance du Québec, it was founded by Raoul Roy, an ex-militant in the Communist Party of Canada. Then there was *L'Indépendance*, published by the RIN and launched in 1962; and the ephemeral *Québec Libre*, put out by the equally ephemeral Front républicain pour l'indépendance. Occasionally, the Catholic journals *Maintenant* (Dominican) and *Relations* (Jesuit) would take a critical stance.

From 1960 onward, these little reviews took the place once occupied by *Cité Libre,* which continued to publish but no longer played the role it had in the time of Duplessis. Journalist Pierre Vallières, who worked with *Cité Libre* at the time and later wrote the independence-movement classic, *White Niggers of America,* tells how he was fired from the magazine in 1964 even though he was co-editor with Jean Pellerin: "[Pierre] Trudeau and [Gérard] Pelletier chose to kill *Cité Libre* rather than see 'their' magazine become a tool in the cause of independence. . . . I had committed the crime of surrendering the magazine to the 'separatists' and 'Marxists'."[13] Indeed, *Cité Libre* became the vehicle for opponents of the statist and nationalist aspects of the Quiet Revolution and several of its editors soon found themselves in Ottawa.

In 1963 there were widespread signs of a generalized disillusionment with the Quiet Revolution. A number of young people calling themselves the Front de libération du Québec (FLQ) and organized in clandestine cells began setting off bombs: the beginnings of an urban terrorism that would continue sporadically until 1970. In the poorer parts of Montreal "social animators" paid by groups as conservative as the Roman Catholic Church began stirring up the once immoveable citizenry, setting up citizens' committees to challenge authority. Then in 1963, *Parti pris,* a political and cultural review, made its appearance. Between October 1963 and summer 1968 the review published fifty-three issues.

Scholars of the period agree on the exceptional importance of this magazine, produced mainly by university students, young artists and poets. Interestingly, the founders and major organizers of *Parti pris* were still at the centre of the action some twenty years later. Some examples: Jean-Marc Piotte, writer, professor and union activist; Paul Chamberland, active in artistic and counter-culture circles; Pierre Maheu, who at the time of his death in 1979 was working on the Quebec government's white paper on sovereignty-association; and Gérald Godin, a PQ cabinet minister. *Parti pris*' press-run never went beyond four thousand copies, but the review is considered nonetheless one of the cornerstones of what later came to be called "the Quebec left".[14]

Parti pris declared itself "pro-independence, socialist and secular", thus clearly distinguishing itself from the reformist current of the Quiet Revolution best represented by the Quebec Liberal Federation. It started as an intellectual experiment whose goal became to unite the incoherent approaches it perceived among the groups and parties springing up around it. According to Roch Denis, its purpose was "to respond to the problems raised by the issues of socialism and the national question".[15] It rejected the reform approach and took a stand in favour of quick and total transformation.

The review's radical positions set it apart from the preceding generation of intellectuals; its social concerns separated it from the mainstream of the independence movement; and its early criticism of the spineless nature of the Quiet Revolution put it one step ahead of the union movement of the time. According to Robert Major, the author of a major work on *Parti pris,* the review was "a true phenomenon of the sixties. It was one example out of many of the arrival of the young generation on the political scene of western countries. In Quebec in particular, it was the perfect incarnation of the gestation of a new society filled with contradictions and bursting everywhere at once."[16] In Major's opinion, the magazines that had preceded *Parti pris* were marginal and without widespread influence in comparison. *Parti pris* replaced the Quiet Revolution ideology of *rattrapage,* or "catching up", with one of self-determination and independence.

As a communications enterprise, *Parti pris* displayed a contagious enthusiasm that left its mark. Its analyses were often criticized as incomplete, premature and sometimes naive, but as a major force in its era the magazine introduced key radical notions at a time when Quebec was in turmoil. It also soon created offspring of its own.

In September 1964 *Révolution québécoise* appeared, founded by journalist Pierre Vallières (recently dismissed from *Cité Libre*), sociologist Charles Gagnon and several others. Vallières comments with irony on the climate of the times: "This review, labelled extreme-left by police, was launched at the house of André Laurendeau [editor-in-chief of Le Devoir]!"[17]

Révolution québécoise published only eight issues over a period lasting less than a year. But that was long enough to set out the parameters of the independence debate within the newly forming Quebec left. The review harshly criticized the *Parti pris* position of "tactical support" for the most popular approach, which favoured the progressive building up of power by the State in Quebec. It also broached some other equally burning questions — such as the role of unions and revolutionary violence — which were then preoccupying the left. When the magazine folded in 1965, its writers rallied to *Parti pris*.

Meanwhile, in the spring of 1964 another group of intellectuals along with a few union activists founded the magazine *Socialisme*, oriented more towards theory and analysis than direct action and organization. *Socialisme*, published on a regular basis up through the beginning of the 1970s, greatly contributed to the creation of a radical intellectual understanding of the Quebec context. The review's appearance was a kind of landmark in the emergence of a Marxist approach to Quebec sociology, a distinct style that was to nourish the social movements of the seventies. It was not only the first forum to place a priority on class analysis, but was also in itself an element in the evolution of class relations. Its impact, too, was much greater than its immediate readership. In fact, *Socialisme* was the ancestor of at least two more recent reviews of a similar nature: *Possibles* and *Les cahiers du socialisme*, both founded in 1978, the first of a self-management, socialist stripe, the second more orthodox in its Marxism.[18]

By 1965, all the intellectual ferment began to seek political outlets. Around the time it absorbed *Révolution québécoise*, *Parti pris* became involved in setting up a new political organization, the Mouvement de libération populaire (MLP — Popular Liberation Movement).

The MLP was marked by endless infighting and intrigue that quickly sapped its energy.[19] One of the key elements of debate centred on the relationship between political organizing and propaganda. The *Parti pris*/MLP experience foreshadowed conflicts on this question that were to dominate Quebec opposition movements after 1972. But already in 1965, debate was spirited. For instance, soon after he was welcomed into *Parti pris,* Charles Gagnon — the future founder of En lutte! (In Struggle), "the political arm of the working class" — was dismissing his new colleagues as "a bunch of armchair revolutionaries".[20]

While *Parti pris* was formally at the heart of a political organization it had helped to found, the ideas it put forth were also beginning to influence other movements like the RIN, whose left wing believed socialism and independence were inseparable for Quebec. But the debates on the left were eclipsed in the fall of 1967 when the nationalist wing of the Quebec Liberal Party split off under the direction of René Lévesque to become the Mouvement Souveraineté-Association (MSA). A year later, the Parti québécois (PQ) was founded, bringing together the MSA, the Ralliement national (a small right-wing nationalist party) and militants from the RIN, which had by then dissolved. The creation of a traditional political party to champion the independence of Quebec brought on a crisis among left-wing nationalist elements. *Parti pris,* for one, would not survive the decision about whether or not to support the PQ. The review published its final issue in the summer of 1968.

The nationalist movement gained legitimacy with the creation of the PQ. For the left, this meant the end of an era during which nationalism had been the major element of its program. Socialists began pulling away from nationalism to develop an autonomous direction politically based on popular and union movements.[21] Independence was still part of the "program" of the left, but it was only one aspect of its overall menu of social transformation. According to Roch Denis' analysis: "From 1968 onward, in search of a way to support national and social struggles, a political alternative matured in the workers' movement . . . and among the young in Quebec. This alternative would bring together in a single program the basic solution to social questions and to the national question."[22] One group of activists formed the short-lived Comité indépendance-socialisme (the Committee for Socialism and Independence); another set up the Front de libération populaire (FLP — literally, "Popular Liberation Front"), a semi-clandestine group that would have a certain influence as a result of the street actions it organized and its publication, *Mobilisation.*

Mobilisation was a direct successor to *Révolution québécoise,* the experiment that had short-circuited five years earlier. It even reprinted its predecessor's most important articles on Quebec politics, class struggle and nationalism. As its name indicates, *Mobilisation* intended to be a tool for mobilizing readers; its goal was to stimulate ideological debate and to provide theoretical education for activists. In its own words, "*Mobilisation* sounds an alarm that will become a battle-cry, a call to involvement."[23]

The review published only five issues between summer 1969 and winter 1970, but FLP members were involved in organizing many of the political campaigns of the time: *McGill Français,* the campaign to turn Quebec's anglophone élite university into a French-speaking institution; the fight against Bill 63, the Quebec government's language law guaranteeing English education rights; and *Opération Libération Vallières-Gagnon,* a campaign to free the two well-known activists then in prison awaiting trial on terrorist-related charges. All of these issues were the object of huge street demonstrations in 1969, and the FLP became one of the favourite targets for the police and legal repression that increased during the same year as conflicts radicalized and hardened. The FLP also published several issues of a tabloid paper called *La Masse,* printed in large quantity and distributed free. It was supposed to be read by "the popular masses", but its influence was less than that of the magazine.

By the end of the summer of 1970, badgered by repression and weakened by internal political strife, the organization dissolved. But *Mobilisation* was to be resurrected some time later by a new generation of militants. (see chapter 4.2.)

The small magazines like *Parti pris* and *Mobilisation* were often seen by their creators as propaganda tools. Yet they might better be considered as forums in which a new culture of protest was being created during the 1960s. Rather than urging a target-population on towards a specific action, as a true propaganda tool would have done, *Parti pris* and the others instilled Quebec youth with a sense of revolt. This was a feeling that would soon spill over into other social arenas, mostly through organizations representing popular and union movements.

3. Traditional media under attack

By 1965-66, a critical distance had developed towards the reformist current of the Quiet Revolution, and this criticism was expressed through increasing social turmoil in all areas. The Liberals, elected in 1960 and re-elected two years later, were dispatched to the opposition benches in June 1966. The Union nationale, Duplessis' old party, came back to power with Daniel Johnson as its leader. But the desire for change had not faded. It had simply changed focus. From 1966 onward, throughout popular, union and nationalist quarters, grassroots voices began to make demands.

Typical of the times was the student movement. The student paper at the University of Montreal, *Le Quartier Latin*, "discovered it was socialist" in 1965. And the following year, Quebec's students' union, l'Union générale des étudiants du Québec (UGEQ), forged an unprecedented link with the workers' movement by inviting CSN president Marcel Pépin to speak at its annual meeting.[24]

In the labour movement, there were signs of a new ideology of politicized unionism based on the notion of class struggle. This sense of conflict took root in the new middle class composed of public-sector employees; it made itself felt in the CSN's increasingly militant declarations. In fact, the wave of discontent that had brought the Union Nationale to power was largely the result of a record number of unresolved strikes. From 1965 to

1967, the idea of peaceful co-existence between unions and government continued to fade and the employer/State resorted to legislated repression on several occasions, including an injunction against professors and hospital workers in 1966 and the passing of special laws against teachers and Montreal Transit Commission employees the following year.[25]

Among the popular movements, the emergence of a socialist alternative struck its first durable roots in the form of citizens' committees that had developed from community organizing experiences.[26] Rather timid at the start, these groups began making specific demands as a way of protesting against the domination of capital and the capitalist State. They ended up being so successful and numerous — it was estimated that two thousand popular groups were created in Quebec after 1965[27] — that the State was forced, some years later, to create a whole series of new structures to pull the rug from under them (see chapter 3.4).

After a period of theorizing and long, exhausting internal struggles, militants of the *Parti pris*/MLP group began to get involved in neighbourhood action. Community organizing, once dominated by private agencies such as the Catholic Church's Conseil des oeuvres de Montréal and McGill University's Urban Social Redevelopment Plan, began to take on a socialist tone. Ironically, one of the most important agencies of this transformation belonged to the federal government — the Company of Young Canadians (CYC).

From 1968 onward, a new type of community group entered the fray, working through collective projects rather than specific demands. Its members created consumers' co-ops and medical clinics in downtown Montreal neighbourhoods, with a major objective being to provide people with information on the scope of their personal or civil rights. The groups hoped that specific projects presented as alternatives to dominant practices would serve as examples of what might be done throughout the society. In practice the question of information often took a back seat to more immediate concerns. As a rule, leadership was left to intellectuals who developed the analyses and set down the goals, strategies and means to be taken — while the populace watched.

Several of the projects launched at this time were specifically tied into information. In the Saint-Henri neighbourhood, militants created POPIR (Projet d'organisation populaire d'information et de regroupement) in an effort to reach and mobilize welfare recipients and the working poor, providing resource-aid to existing groups. In the Saint-Louis neighbourhood, where a new generation of disaffected young people was settling, some of the "educated unemployed" (a category created by the school reforms of the Quiet Revolution) started the Atelier-Communication project, offering printing, research and organizational services. Wherever community organizing had taken hold, activists began establishing communication networks that reflected the ideology of participation and protest that characterized the new popular groups. The accent was placed on local information.

At the same time, on various fronts a movement of political consolidation was taking shape. On March 19, 1968, a meeting of Montreal citizens' committees took place with the purpose of establishing links and undertaking a common socio-political action. Shortly thereafter, the CSN took on a new responsibility: Recognizing the limits of action based solely on the negotiation of collective agreements, the central opened a "second front", to work on issues such as the quality of life, on consumers' interests and on general political action. In his state-of-the-union report to the CSN convention in 1968, president Marcel Pépin admitted that the union movement was no longer in the avant-garde of society.[28] He stressed the importance of the type of political action being practised by citizens' and action committees, which had been bringing together wage-earners on a neighbourhood basis since 1966. Pépin declared that the union movement had to enlarge its field of interest.

One of the key elements of Pépin's report was a denunciation of the "scandal of the information media."[29] The mass media, in most cases owned by big capital, are run like commercial enterprises, Pépin pointed out. They are designed to make the most profit possible, and thus have to favour advertising over public-interest information. Journalists suffer from a lack of professional tools and freedom, while editorial policy defends the capitalist system and the authorities. As a result, social agents whose points of view oppose the system are denied access to media, further exploiting the citizens who consume these forms of information.

This was the first time an individual of such high office, the president of a major union central, had denounced the role of the traditional media so vigorously. Since the union movement should be striving for an independent critical stance towards the current regime, Pépin went on, the movement and its supporters should undertake ideological action using, among other means, popular information:

> We're up against spoken and written media that serve their owners, and we can't overestimate how much these media maintain the system of exploitation. The CSN realizes it has to start building popular means of information, to counterbalance the influence of the information media that, by their very ownership, are committed to the interests of the ruling classes.[30]

According to Pépin, the CSN's publications and the union structures could provide "the beginnings of a free information system, dedicated to the working classes". But there was a lot of work ahead.[32]

Public opinion was alerted to the question of media when, in December 1968, Liberal MNA Yves Michaud spoke to the Quebec National Assembly about corporate concentration in the press.* In the spring of 1969, Jean-Jacques Bertrand's Union Nationale government set up a Special Parliamentary Commission on freedom of the press. The commission never did publish any conclusions or recommendations, but the eighteen briefs it received constitute an interesting bit of documentation on the issue. Journalists, newspapers, individuals, unions and professional organizations appeared before the commission, and all of them — except for the newspaper companies themselves, of course — denounced the lack of real freedom of information that

---

* Yves Michaud would later become editor of the pro-sovereignty daily *Le Jour*. See chapter 4.5.

was created by the private enterprise system in the newspaper sector. [32]

Opponents of the status quo realized that the Quebec press could not offer politically useful information. As far as the public sector was concerned — essentially Radio-Canada — the situation was not much better. The Radio-Canada newsroom, one of the key pockets of opposition to the Duplessis regime towards the end of the 1950s, was called upon to play a different role once Canada's "national unity" was challenged, although many of its journalists were openly sympathetic to the cause of Quebec independence. [33] After 1968, the atmosphere was tense in the newsroom, as word came down from above that the growing protests were to be granted minimum coverage. When the annual Saint-Jean-Baptiste Day parade turned into a riot, on June 24, 1968 Radio-Canada's cameras remained resolutely focused on the traditional procession as demonstrators and police fought it out two feet away. The cameras were forced to record the fact that something was amiss only when a thrown bottle narrowly missed hitting Prime Minister Trudeau, watching from the reviewing stand on the eve of his first election. [34]

At *La Presse* during the night following this demonstration, news director Pierre Lafrance and a member of the board of directors, Jean Parisien, personally inspected all news articles and put together the front page, a most unusual interference from above, in a metropolitan daily. [35] Their work supported the action of the local police. In the years to follow, this type of "committed" journalism was to become common in Quebec, especially as an increasingly difficult social climate caused the breakdown of "objective" journalistic practices that are the norm in calmer times.

The public soon became aware of the media's total submission to private enterprise and/or the State. Different opposition groups saw it too, and tried to put forward their own vision of Quebec society. Using this awareness, the protest movement made various attempts to take control of communication between 1969 and 1972.

INDEPENDENT MEDIA: THE ALTERNATIVES

As social tensions heightened in Quebec towards the end of the 1960s, opposition groups realized how badly they needed a system of communication to express their own political voice. This need was to be stated in different ways at different times by a variety of groups and, as a result, the years between 1969 and 1972 witnessed a stream of important experiences in alternative communications.

Two types of expression are especially pertinent to this study. On one hand, a number of organized social groups took the initiative to create and operate their own independent means of communication. This included, for instance, the publication of the weekly *Québec-Presse* (1969-1974) and the work of L'Agence de presse libre du Québec — literally, "the Quebec Free Press Agency" (1971-1976). On the other hand — and perhaps more dramatic — was the move by some activists towards the direct takeover of communications during times of social unrest, such as the October Crisis of 1970 and the first general strike of public sector workers in 1972.

1. Québec-Presse: a popular response to cultural domination

"FIVE DIE AT RIVIÈRE-DU-LOUP" cried the headline of the first issue of *Québec-Presse,* October 19, 1969. It was the kind of head that would be rare in the paper, and it immediately revealed a contradiction in the goals of the new weekly.

Québec-Presse professed to want to both penetrate the mass market and to offer a content that would be different from mainstream papers. It defined itself as a "national popular" publication dedicated to "free" information. The front page of that same maiden issue hinted at what was inside: "Who killed Corporal Dumas?"* "The police step up raids." "Miners occupy American gold mine in Bolivia." And so on. . . .

Québec-Presse intended to be different not only in its content, but also in organization and finances. Set up as a co-operative, it recruited its members from unions, popular groups, credit unions, other co-ops and democratic movements. The three major union organizations — Confédération des syndicats nationaux (CSN); Fédération des travailleurs du Québec (FTQ); Centrale de l'enseignement du Québec (CEQ) — played a key role in its founding. But the Association coopérative des publications populaires, created for the occasion in October 1969, was really a coalition of three types of groups represented in more or less equal proportion: the workers' movement and popular and union organizations; the nationalist movement; and the student and university sector.[1] Journalists held the majority on the editorial committee.

From its first issue, the paper covered subjects previously taboo in the rest of the mass media. There were articles on the growing opposition to Mayor Jean Drapeau's regime in Montreal; on the wave of searches and raids directed by police against citizens' committees; on the city administration's campaign against the Company of Young Canadians. Every week the front page discussed the latest developments in national and social conflicts. It was a politically hot autumn, and *Québec-Presse* reported in full detail how the representatives of Quebec justice had seized the books of radical essayists Pierre Vallières and Pierre Vadeboncoeur. The weekly also generously covered demonstrations such as those by French-unilingualists against Bill 63 on language rights and by taxi drivers against the Murray Hill

* Corporal Robert Dumas was an undercover policeman from the Quebec provincial police who was killed by a gunshot during a demonstration on October 7, 1969.

company's airport monopoly. It reported on the campaign to free political prisoners Vallières and Charles Gagnon and on the imprisonment of union leader Michel Chartrand, charged with sedition. For the first time, partisans of social movements could read in-depth articles and get trustworthy information on a regular basis.

In the spring following its founding, the paper laid out its objectives in a lengthy declaration of principles:

> *Québec-Presse* is the people's response to the domination of the press by cultural, political or economic dictatorship, or by the private interests that support such a dictatorship.
> *Québec-Presse* is a journal of information and struggle . . . a free and involved newspaper. It is entirely independent of the capitalist forces dominating society, and it intends to act in concert with the aspirations of the people and their organizations.[2]

The declaration went on to state that the paper would support those elements of society protesting the power and control of the financial establishment, bourgeoisie and other capitalist forces. If it criticized popular initiatives and organizations, it would do so only "with the people's aspirations in mind". The paper recognized Quebec's right to self-determination. It would guarantee the "professional freedom" of its own journalists and retain independence from all political parties, supporting none "currently compromised by participation in the system". It reserved the right, however, "to support any political party not tied to capitalist interests, whose structure and function are democratic, and whose program is in accord with the aspirations of the Quebec people".

"Above all," the declaration stated, "*Québec-Presse* works towards its objectives by providing accurate information that sheds light on what the authorities attempt to keep hidden."

Despite its obvious good will, *Québec-Presse* had the problems inherent to any project trying to function within the dominant system — or on its margins — without following the rules of the game. The paper did not want to be commercial, but it still had to be self-financing. A few months after its launching, it sent out its first appeal for funds. *Québec-Presse* needed $100,000 and five thousand new subscribers.[3]

In April 1970, editor-in-chief Jacques Guay quit his job over disagreements with the paper's news policy; his point of view was in the minority. "Under the guise of not wanting to practise classical journalism," he declared in a statement published by the paper, "the current group is foundering in sensationalism and meaninglessness."[4] Financial problems continued to plague the weekly. The very day of Guay's departure, the finance campaign's goal rose to $300,000. Eventually, in order to reach a mass-market audience, *Québec-Presse* was forced to turn its distribution over to services controlled by monopolies such as Power Corporation and Québécor. Besides directly contradicting its own declaration of principles, this step created obvious problems for continued economic control, especially in a time of rising production costs and inflation.[5] The lack of funds was a constant source of worry until the paper finally had to close on November 10, 1974, after 252 issues and five years on the newsstands.

But especially between 1970 and 1972, *Québec-Presse* was an indispensible source of information on the evolution of different social movements. It was particularly crucial during periods of crisis, such as October 1970 and the 1972 Common Front strikes in the public sector. Activists of the period considered that *Québec-Presse* belonged to them, and the people involved with the paper felt that way too.

Québec-Presse was the only paper in Quebec to publish the manifesto of the Front de libération du Québec (FLQ) several months before the outbreak of the October Crisis, in June of 1970. In September of the same year, to celebrate Labour Day it published a supplement on workers in Quebec. In October 1970, in addition to exemplary coverage of events, it gave editorial support to the FLQ's analysis, adding that *Québec-Presse* saw itself as carrying out the same struggle — for the liberation of Quebec — but by other means, namely through information.[6] It not only reported but also underwent the political and legal repression of October. Not surprisingly, as its second year began the paper discovered it was being boycotted by advertisers, business-men and public institutions.

From the paper's beginnings, a general assembly of its members had determined content. In October 1972 the assembly criticized the writers and reoriented the paper's priorities. From then on, emphasis was to be put on municipal politics, the women's movement, consumer protection and regional news. Since social movements were evolving, the paper had to follow suit.

Québec-Presse had to be taken seriously by the ruling class as well. Every Saturday night, as the paper was rolling off the press, a liveried chauffeur in a government limousine would show up at the printer's and pick up several copies. Popular rumour had it that these were then delivered directly to the home of Premier Robert Bourassa.[8]

But there were outside obstacles to be faced. On the paper's third birthday its editor, Gérald Godin, accused the provincial and federal governments of "economic censorship". He said the authorities were not purchasing the appropriate amount of advertising in *Québec-Presse*; they were refusing to spend the percentage of their budgets that was proportionally justified by the paper's circulation.[9] In Godin's opinion, this was the major barrier to the profits that would make expansion possible.

Québec-Presse always remained linked to the union organizations (CSN-FTQ-CEQ) that had helped found it; the tie lasted through its five-year lifespan.[10] But in some minds *Québec-Presse* was still just "a big nationalist weekly" with an insufficient base in the working class.[11] During the public sector general strike of 1972, for example, radical militants occupied the printing plant, demanding the elimination of a regular column by economist Jacques Parizeau — at the time an executive member of the Parti québécois (see also chapter 3.7). Other critics considered the paper full of good intentions but destined to fail for lack of ties to a political organization.[12]

The paper was bound not to last. In 1974 the coalition that had founded *Québec-Presse* began to dissolve. On the union front, there was rivalry between the major centrals, a competition reflected within the paper itself. It did not help that this was also the time of the Cliche Commission, whose inquiry into union activities in the construction industry made inter-union relations more difficult. At the same time the nationalist movement had its energies diverted towards the new daily *Le Jour,* launched in February. Then there were those eternal financial worries. They were the straw that broke *Québec-Presse*'s back.

The end came on November 10, 1974. Yet the experience was a positive one. The very existence, even temporary, of *Québec-Presse* proved to Normand Caron that "There was unity and solidarity within the forces working for change in Quebec."[13] *Québec-Presse*, an attempt to create "free information", left its mark on Quebec social movements. The effect it had on building an alternative culture cannot be overestimated.[14]

When it went under, the *Québec-Presse* co-op had some two thousand members and the paper sold just under 30,000 copies per issue. At its high point in October 1970 total copies sold reached 52,000. By comparison, in 1974 *Le Devoir* was publishing 42,500 copies and *Le Jour* 30,000.

The void left by the paper's demise was felt even into the 1980s. A group of communication workers, moved by this sense of absence, decided to publish a commemorative edition of *Québec-Presse* for May Day 1981. Among other things the issue contained a complete assessment of how *Québec-Presse* functioned and was financed. The purpose of this new effort went beyond nostalgia and was seen as an attempt to revive the idea of a national left-wing weekly.[15]

2. FRAP: movement without a messenger

The launching of *Québec-Presse* had been an attempt to break ruling-class hegemony over information in Quebec, but its period of publication was also marked by a series of political actions. From the first issues on, the weekly included articles on new attempts to channel the energies of opposition groups.[16]

As early as September 1969, community and popular-group activists had contacted the full-time organizers of the Montreal Central Council, the regional level of the CSN that had been talking of a "second front" for the past year. Between November 1969 and March 1970, eight political action committees saw the light of day in various Montreal neighbourhoods, as a result of co-operation between unions and community groups. During the summer of 1970 these action committees decided to enter the municipal elections due that fall. They launched the Front d'action politique des salariés (literally the "Workers' Political Action Front"), otherwise known as FRAP. Legitimated by this decision to participate in official electoral politics, the popular movement began to attract attention in the mass media. It also achieved a certain notoriety: Newspapers, *Le Devoir* in particular, described how city councillors refused to appear before public meetings organized by FRAP.

FRAP was counting on both the formal and informal communication networks existing in various neighbourhoods. It based its support on the sense of belonging to a new common political culture — a sense that was emerging with the help of tools such as *Québec-Presse*. It relied as well on union information networks and mass media coverage. However, only the mass media were able to offer the kind of exposure necessary to a movement intending to run in an election. Without realizing it, FRAP became dependent on the mass media: this was a relationship it could never control. And because FRAP never did establish an independent means of communicating directly with the population, it was destined to fail.

When the October Crisis broke only three weeks before the election, confusion and division reigned within FRAP, while the authorities found a golden opportunity to discredit the opposition. FRAP both condemned the FLQ's actions and supported its analysis of society. The mass media found this position to be ambiguous and unclear, and reacted with universal reprobation. On the other hand Montreal mayor Jean Drapeau — following the FLQ's lead — was able to establish his own direct means of communication. After the War Measures Act went into effect, Drapeau went on every media outlet willing to have him — private radio stations mostly — to address the populace about the connections between FRAP and the FLQ. A victim of its dependency relationship with the media, FRAP became lost in the shuffle, along with its message.

When it came time for the municipal elections, FRAP reaped some 20 per cent of the vote in the areas where its candidates ran. Its downfall cannot be attributed solely to the October Crisis, though the events certainly did cost it several percentage points. FRAP's fate was unavoidable, for it tried to engage in political action without building its own clearly defined communication strategy.

3. October 1970: direct communication (1)

The Front de libération du Québec, or FLQ, situated its action in the same general context as FRAP. But the FLQ took direct control of communication and used the media as an integral element of its overall strategy. Though it was not rewarded with political success, the FLQ succeeded for a time in publicly imposing a counter-interpretation of social reality, and did so on a grand scale. It took the traditional mass media relay stations of established power and turned them against themselves. By doing so, the FLQ accomplished an act of cultural communication that would have long-lasting results. Social movements comparing the experiences of FRAP and the FLQ could not help asking themselves a few questions about policies and strategies. Questions about communication figured high on the list.

The initials FLQ do not stand for a homogeneous group with a linear history. Rather, the acronym was adopted at different times by unrelated small groups of militants involved in various social actions, people who decided to perform spectacular acts in order to step up the rhythm of conflict. This was the spirit behind the first mailbox bombings in 1963, as well as behind the waves of militant action that followed in 1965-66 and 1968-69. But, although the different FLQs were able to publicize nationalist and popular demands up to a certain point, these demands were never placed directly before the mass audience of media consumers until October 1970.[17]

The Liberals had returned to power under Robert Bourassa in April 1970, but this was no cause for celebration in opposition circles. A general indifference towards "official" politics — much of it resulting from the fact that in the 1970 election the Parti québécois won 24 per cent of the vote but acquired only seven seats in the legislature — set the stage for extra-parliamentary action. The crisis began on Monday, October 5, when the British commercial attaché James Cross was kidnapped in Montreal. It was later discovered that the kidnappers had been active in social movements of the time, especially among taxi drivers and student groups.

Some writers contend that the October Crisis was, among other things, a struggle for temporary control of Quebec's communication system — an hypothesis worth examining.[18] Through its sophisticated understanding of the public's mood, the wheels of power and especially the intermediary role of the mass media, the FLQ was able to impose its own information strategy and create new channels through which it could *directly* communicate with the population. As a result, official information sources were "caught in their own trap", to quote a commentator of the time.[19]

The FLQ had the momentum from the start. By sending its communiqués to private radio stations, it was assured of a dramatic presentation. The FLQ bet that the system of competition and profit would work in its favour and it was right.[20] To create its own forms of communication, the FLQ's strategy was to place two private Montreal radio stations — CKAC and CKLM — in competition with each other to see which could deliver the "breaking news" first. In this way the FLQ "forced the media to open its doors" and spoke directly to the population, something that could not be done by exploding bombs. For the FLQ, this was one of the major goals of the whole enterprise. In the opinion of political scientist Arthur Siegel, who did an intensive study of press coverage of the October Crisis, the FLQ was extremely shrewd in its choice of radio as the medium to present its message. Radio is particularly well adapted to broadcasting a text quickly, thus avoiding the kind of censorship likely to happen in television, for instance.[21]

One of the main demands of the British diplomat's kidnappers was that radio and television transmit the FLQ's manifesto, and that newspapers publish it. Strangely enough, that demand was the only one the authorities gave in to. There is no doubt that the broadcast of the manifesto over Radio-Canada's television network on Thursday, October 8, was a great victory, not only for the FLQ, but for the very notion of counter-information. The manifesto is an extraordinary document, questioning received ideas by *naming a reality other* than the one usually transmitted through the media.[22]

The story of the intrigue in government circles and the press preceding the decision to broadcast the manifesto is a fascinating one.[23] During the first few days of the Crisis, the Montreal media's complacent attitude towards the events brought down the wrath of Pierre Trudeau. For a short time, Trudeau considered asking the cabinet to impose official censorship.[24] Meanwhile, at Radio-Canada, all systems were ready for broadcasting the manifesto on Wednesday evening, but a counter-order directly from Trudeau's office, made after a consultation with the cabinet, put off the decision.[25] However, later that night, the manifesto was read on radio station CKAC by journalist Louis Fournier. Meanwhile, at *La Presse*, the manifesto was typeset overnight, but the next morning, after a midnight telephone call to owner Paul Desmarais from Marc Lalonde, then Trudeau's chief advisor, the news editor gave the order not to publish the text. Early Thursday evening, *Montréal-Matin* announced it would be publishing the manifesto the next day, come what may. Marc Lalonde called the daily but it was no dice, the paper wouldn't give in.[26]

In Ottawa, realizing it would be impossible to block broadcast of the manifesto in the Quebec media, Trudeau gave the order to the television network of Radio-Canada to let it roll. According to *Last Post* magazine, this was a sign proving how sure the Prime Minister was that the manifesto would receive a negative reaction from viewers because of its "extreme" language.[27] Secretary of State Gérard Pelletier apparently told parliamentary journalists in Ottawa that there was nothing to fear because the text was "stupid".[28] On Thursday evening at 10:30

— the time Radio-Canada usually ran its news — "for humanitarian reasons" the network broadcast the complete FLQ manifesto. Friday morning, every French-language newspaper in Montreal carried it.

The manifesto's publication did not have the effect foreseen by federal politicans. According to the staff of the *Last Post*:

Its language was simple, the grievances it pointed to were real, and much of it gained wide support. . . .

A survey of opinions on hot-line programs on popular French stations in Montreal showed that the vast majority of callers condemned the actual acts of the FLQ, but over 50 per cent supported the spirit of the manifesto.

A CBC interviewer took a survey in front of a French Catholic church after 11 o'clock mass on Sunday, and found that condemnation of the acts was almost universal, but that half the people he talked to expressed sympathy for the things said in the FLQ manifesto.[29]

The manifesto's broadcast gave the FLQ a kind of popular support it could never have garnered based on action alone. The manifesto spoke of social ills in Quebec in direct and straightforward language and hit its mark. In a special editorial, the *Québec-Presse* committee wrote:

The same authorities denounced by the FLQ took it upon themselves to speak for the majority and condemn this week's terrorist acts. That doesn't mean much in itself. . . . The only argument that counts is the one the people make. The FLQ knew how to speak to them as never before. The FLQ's actions have been a kind of crash course in politicization by total immersion. . . . The FLQ reached its main goal: to speak to the world in its own words. And to make the *Québécois* aware of their own situation.[30]

Between October 5 and October 9, 1970, the FLQ was able to influence the communications system directly and impose a counter-interpretation of social reality on public consciousness. Caught off-guard, the political authorities had to react quickly to regain control of communications.

It was hard catching up. On Saturday, October 10, Quebec's Justice Minister Jérôme Choquette gave a live televised press conference to parade his hard line against the FLQ's demands. His speech may have helped re-establish public trust in the government's ability to control the situation. But ten minutes after Choquette's press conference, a second FLQ cell kidnapped provincial cabinet minister Pierre Laporte in front of his suburban Montreal house. As one thing led to another in this way, the FLQ was able to maintain its advantage in the communications game, in defining the rules and forcing new types of action on traditional media, especially the radio.[31] Even Gérard Pelletier ended up admitting how successful the FLQ's strategy really was, and how popular the group was up until Laporte's death. The FLQ, it seemed, was able to draw the government into one trap after another.[32]

But at least one conventional newspaper went beyond the usual role of bilateral communications channel (between the authorities and the FLQ) and tried to play a more dynamic role and participate in the Crisis. This was *Le Devoir*, an independent daily with a long history of taking stands in public affairs.

From the time the Crisis began, Claude Ryan, *Le Devoir*'s editor and publisher, tried to play a political role above and beyond what he published in the paper. He called a number of influential public figures together with the idea of convincing the provincial government to talk to the FLQ and obtain the safe release of the hostages. The group, which became known as "Quebec's wise men" and included René Lévesque, Marcel Pépin of the CSN, Louis Laberge of the FTQ and Yvon Charbonneau of the CEQ, issued a public declaration urging the Quebec government to negotiate.

At the same time Ryan's paper gave neutral coverage to the events, coverage that by its very neutrality appeared conciliatory to the FLQ. Ryan proved he knew exactly how influential the media could be in times of crisis, whereas other communicators were less perspicacious.[33] *Le Devoir* actually gave proportionally thirty times more space to the Crisis than did *La Presse*.[34]

During the second week of the Crisis, the authorities realized that they could no longer hope to exercise political control over the situation, given that they had completely lost control of communications. On October 16 the federal government proclaimed a state of martial law under the War Measures Act. The day before, the Canadian army had already begun in effect to occupy Quebec, and especially Montreal. As well as letting the government mop up all sections of the protest movement in Quebec, the War Measures Act allowed the authorities to re-establish control over the dynamics of news dissemination. Arthur Siegel, in his university thesis on mass media and the October Crisis, arrives at a similar conclusion:

> If the October Crisis is viewed in one sense as a battle for temporary control of the communications system in Quebec, then it may be argued that the FLQ had reached its high point of power with the statement of support for a negotiated deal by the Quebec "wise men". After that came the War Measures Act, which in effect limited the freedom of the media to act as a communications channel for the FLQ. It is indeed likely that *Le Devoir*'s position played a role in helping the government decide that the time had come to invoke the War Measures Act and the accompanying emergency measures. [35]

The War Measures Act brought with it the suspension of civil liberties and summary arrests on suspicion of having committed retroactive crimes. But more importantly, it blocked the communications channels that the FLQ had established. It forbade the media to publish news about the FLQ unless that news came from the authorities. The media no longer had the right to publish communiqués, or even admit they had received them. Instead of the direct information of the two preceding weeks — instead of the usual "freedom of information" routine (which in any case means information selected according to criteria established by the media industry) — public authorities dictated who would speak. Quebec justice minister Choquette declared: "In this very special case, in the public interest, freedom of the press must be curtailed." [36]

The October Crisis was a turning point in relations between the opposition and the authorities. It became obvious how effective direct communication could be. The importance of the mass media in maintaining the *status quo* and the crucial role of communications control in times of crisis became clear to everyone involved.

The Crisis was over. But the FLQ's style forced political action groups to question their attitudes towards mass media.[37] A political evaluation done by the editorial team at *Socialisme québécois* was perhaps typical. The journal recognized the success of the FLQ in getting its manifesto broadcast and in raising up the sympathy and awareness of the working class. But it questioned the ultimate legacy of the action:

> It is undeniable that a movement of explicit or tacit approval was felt all across Quebec. However, politics and class struggle are not carried out by either real or potential awareness. They are made by equal and unequal power relations and most often these relations make themselves felt through organization.[38]

To put it simply, activists wondered which path they should choose. The FLQ cells had used the official information system for their own ends, but at what price? *Québec-Presse* was competing against that system on its own ground, but how efficient was it? Was the launching of a parallel information network anything more than a pipe dream? These were the issues in counter-information — and in political information per se — at the start of the 1970s.

The recent evolution of Quebec's capitalist press, with its corporate concentration and ideological reinforcement, made it clear that the press could never be systematically used to transmit the ideas of social movements. The constant ideological control exercised by business; self-censorship practised by journalists afraid of pressure and reprisals; the limits to tolerance of criticism; the emphasis on description over explanation; the shift in power from the unions to press conglomerates: Those factors made it clear that mass media could never be turned against ruling-class interests.

The FLQ did succeed in taking control of the media through the spectacular nature of its action. But it was another story when a popular group wanted to hold a press conference. As the anonymous journalist "B.R." put it: "If you decide to opt for comprehensibility and use mass-media language, you reduce the political content of your statement. But if you use political language, once it goes into the capitalist information system, it ends up losing its meaning.[39]

Around this time activists began seeing the issue of information as a question of ideological struggle, tied to economic and political battles, and it became obvious that they had to find new forms of organization, which would bring these different aspects together in a common effort.

4. Social integration: the state responds

The October Crisis necessitated adjustments on the part of all of Quebec's social movements. The Crisis revealed that the federal State, the repressive arm of the political and economic system, had no scruples when it came to preserving the status quo. Within the nationalist movement, this realization reinforced the hegemony of the Parti québécois, the only officially legitimate expression of nationalism. The union movement saw its field of activity limited to negotiating collective agreements — contract negotiations were approved exercises according to the rules of the game. But for the young and vulnerable popular movements the repression following the Crisis caused major realignments and the emergence of new forms of action, especially in communications.

The community groups created between 1968 and 1970 continued functioning after the October Crisis. Their spirit had been radicalized, but they were also more realistic about just how far the establishment was prepared to go. After 1970 the State began to outflank social movements (through project grants, social services and the like) as the authorities worked to create their own apparatuses of cultural and ideological support.[40]

The social conflicts that culminated in the massive repression of October 1970 forced federal and provincial levels of the State into readjustment. In 1971, the federal government inaugurated two job-creation programs, Opportunities for Youth (OFY) and Local Initiative Projects (LIP). Both were designed to stave off social tensions and co-opt struggles by "buying off" potential young troublemakers.[41]

Meanwhile, on the provincial level, the Quebec government was preparing a major reform of social services (the Castonguay Reform), which was to lead to the creation of Regional Health and Social Service Councils (CRSSS) and Local Community Services Centres (CLSC). This reform integrated the demands of citizens' committees and popular groups into the State apparatus. The results were inevitable: Community organizations controlled by local populations either disappeared or became meaningless. Many former community organizers and activists were integrated into the para-public service, becoming "professional militants" along the way.

Yet in spite of all that, between 1970 and 1972 a number of groups were created that were able to avoid State control and remain under the control of activists, users and union and community groups. Some were specifically tied to communications: the Centre de formation populaire (CFP — or "Popular Education Centre"), Centre coopératif de recherche en politique sociale (CCRPS — "Co-operative Centre for Social Policy Research"), Centre de recherche et d'information sur le Québec (CRIQ — "Centre for Research and Information on Quebec"), and the Agence de presse libre du Québec (APLQ).

During these years, State intervention, especially by the Quebec government, was massive and all-inclusive. Since the "participatory" experiments in regional development of the early and mid-1960s (such as the BAEQ — Bureau d'aménagement de l'est du Québec), a series of socio-cultural and educational initiatives with a similar perspective had taken place. The TEVEC program, launched in 1967 in the Lac Saint-Jean area, linked communications and community organizing in an attempt to provide formal adult education through television. In 1970, inspired by this experience, the Quebec ministry of education launched the Multi-media program, which was supposed to "de-school education" by transforming people's attitudes. All of these projects were designed to be controlled by the local populations concerned. As was Radio-Québec, the public television network established in 1968 by the Quebec government in its ongoing communications battle against Ottawa.[42]

These projects, however, were essentially ways to promote the system by using the ideology of access to mass media and the expectations they create. The lack of popular control over the orientation and use of Radio-Québec was denounced by, among others, the Institut canadien d'éducation des adultes (ICEA):

> One thing justifies Radio-Québec's existence: It must be an instrument serving collectivities and controlled by them, so that television can play a true social role. Radio-Québec must do more than bring élite culture into people's homes. It must become a way for local communities to express themselves, a collective promotional instrument for the popular majority.[43]

One study even concludes that the situation had actually regressed from the launching of BAEQ down through the TEVEC and Multi-media projects.[44] These projects, so this study contends, were more concerned with technocratic and bureaucratic needs than with those they purported to be promoting. At other times they were openly diverted to serve the political ends of government or regional and local élites. The population never had any real decision-making power, which is why government participation always brought with it protest from the most aware community groups.

In a certain sense, the community television stations played a more important role as intermediary links in popular struggles. These projects often introduced young people to research practices and techniques which they would later use in community groups and in working to form new protest movements.[45] But just as often, the projects were ways of integrating and co-opting others who would forever remain allies of the State apparatus, often without realizing it.

When they were not already integral parts of government programs, community media were often financed by LIP and OFY grants, or by grants from the Quebec ministry of communications. In some cases, despite these constraints, they were able to make a contribution in the direction of social transformation. In the early 1980s, in a context different from that in which they were created, community media enjoyed a respectable position among alternative communication practices. But ten years earlier the contradictions of government sponsorship undermined the efforts of social movements to create independent means of communication. A group of researchers from France commented:

> In Quebec we did not encounter a single group that was financially independent. Either their material belonged to the ministry of communications, or their organizers survived only thanks to LIP, OFY or other temporary grants. These days in Europe, where the tradition of State intervention in the socio-cultural area is an old one, we are witnessing totally self-sufficient, politically active video groups. But in Quebec, in North America, the home of free enterprise, granting agencies operate systematically.... The weakness of Quebec's social organization ... lets the State reinforce its control over opposition groups that have but slim chances of financing themselves.[46]

This dependence made free channels all the more valuable, although in Quebec no one could agree on what really constituted "community media". Two authors, France Filiatrault and Gaétan Tremblay, compiled a list of these experiences and decided: "In Quebec we've got the habit of pasting the label 'community' or 'popular' on a whole group of communications experiments that often don't have anything in common."[47] These authors' criterion for inclusion in community media was the stated desire to promote alternatives to mainstream media. In their study, done in 1976, they managed to identify fifteen magazines and newspapers, forty-three television and radio stations and fourteen "network" type activities (such as the APLQ), all of which they believed to qualify as community media.

Before 1970, when people in the protest movement spoke of independent means of communication, they did so in relation to privately-controlled media. But from 1971 onward, as the State began to intrude in the "community" communications area, the analysis had to be readjusted to take government involvement into account. Communication networks that truly belonged to protest movements were rare indeed.

5. Networking: the Agence de presse libre du Québec

In the post-October 1970 climate, with the State getting ready to enter community media, the time was right for a second independent means of communication in Quebec: the Agence de presse libre du Québec (APLQ — the Quebec Free Press Agency).

From the very start the APLQ intended to be more radical than *Québec-Presse*; the politics of the times demanded it. The agency's founders were former members of *Quartier Latin*, the popular youth magazine of the late 1960s, which had grown out of the University of Montreal student newspaper of the same name. The APLQ also involved a few professional journalists who had gotten together after the October Crisis. The agency moved into the *Quartier Latin*'s offices.

There were several factors behind the decision to create a news agency. First, the decision was practical: The agency demanded a minimum of initial investment and operating funds, which meant the enterprise could be started at once. At first the agency needed little more than photocopied sheets stapled together. But there were strategic, political factors as well. Through its form and distribution the APLQ was aiming at objectives different than those of a newspaper or review:

> We are not a newspaper.... We are addressing ourselves to groups, newspapers, unions, and not individuals.... Joining the agency means taking a collective stand for free information in Quebec and for the circulation of that information among those creating it.[48]

The APLQ's aim was not simply to reach a politicized élite. Its major goal was to build a communication and information network across Quebec. The agency's founders believed that such a network already existed on an informal basis; their challenge was to render it operational. "We will work to transmit a kind of information that, in a variety of ways, will lead to a true understanding of today's Quebec, information that will inform those involved in transforming their society," said an early *Bulletin*.[49]

In a much more conscious way than *Québec-Presse*, the APLQ worked to bring solidarity to the disparate branches of the movement. Every subscriber was expected to be a participant, to give scattered militants a sense of belonging to a common cause, without necessarily backing a specific political platform. A participant learned about other struggles, distributed information on his or her own movement and helped build the network. From the beginning, special care was taken to cover all regions of Quebec. This turned out to be an easier task than with a conventional newspaper, since the actors themselves were supposed to provide the news. The Agency did not have to use journalists and correspondents.

The Agency's first *Bulletin* appeared in mid-March of 1971. Early issues featured articles on consumer co-ops, housing, municipal democracy, unemployment, the situation in Quebec's junior colleges, a visit by Indochinese women, political action in Rouyn-Noranda, the stormy atmosphere in the newsroom of Sherbrooke's *La Tribune,* as well as international news, community announcements and various studies.

The Agency's importance lay in its role as a liaison and information channel for the popular movement. Contrary to a medium competing in the market-place, like *Québec-Presse,* its success did not depend on the mood of an amorphous "public". Once its subscription list was established — stabilized at around 200 — the Agency was free to concentrate on its service and long-term goals.

Early in 1972 the *Bulletin* took on a handsome new look, thanks to some modern equipment. The publication began to pop up on specialized newsstands. In the second to last issue before its first birthday, the Agency published a supplement entitled *L'information et la lutte* ("Information and Struggle"), in which it set down its goals and the meaning of its involvement:

The APLQ is working to
— launch a free national information network based on local, regional and popular sources;
— circulate information on popular organizations, political action groups and on struggles in Quebec and abroad;
— learn more about the conditions of conflict by studying the evolution of different situations and distributing analyses and teaching documents. . . .

In the information sector, the first task is to combat capitalist ideology transmitted by commercial media. Workers, popular organizations and political action groups rarely have the opportunity to express themselves in these so-called informational media. Yet what they have to say is of fundamental importance.[50]

The APLQ defined its role as a distribution and information tool designed to be a "channel of information about the work and organization of what we broadly refer to as the popular movements". It was self-managed, depended solely on subscribers' fees, and addressed itself to groups rather than individuals:

> Given the current situation, it is important to define an overall information strategy, a way of working by which popular organizations, political action groups, unions, self-defence organizations and non-organized workers can create their own means of information and consciously make use of the ones supplied by the system.
>
> In the long run, this strategy should result in the creation of a truly free and committed information network, expressing the interests and demands of the majority of workers and organizations struggling against the current political and economic system.[51]

This text is important in its recognition of the role of a communications strategy which includes both setting up independent information media and using existing means. Without compromising its political position, the Agency remained committed to an open, self-managing popular movement. As a keystone in this strategy, the APLQ regularly reported on attempts throughout Quebec to invent new types of information aimed at fulfilling particular needs, without falling into any form of political and economic control.

Thus in the pages of the *Bulletin* a reader could find out about such experiments in the information field as the *Journal populaire* in Trois-Rivières, *La Lutte* in Rimouski, *En plein coeur* in Drummondville and *Résistance* in Saint-Jérôme, as well as neighbourhood papers in Montreal such as *Le Critique* in Pointe Saint-Charles and *Le Va Vite* (Downtown-South). The *Bulletin* also reported on the publication of little papers in union locals: *La Strappe* (teachers), *La Voi . . . Libre* (road workers), *l'Engrenage* (bus workers), *Le Q-lotté* (civil servants). The APLQ wrote about regional conflicts over information issues as well as about conflicts in conventional media.[52]

The APLQ also reported on the major workers' struggles of 1972. It attracted the attention of the repressive apparatus and on October 7, 1972, a mysterious burglary took place at its offices. More than one thousand files disappeared. The mystery lingered for several years, until it was revealed in 1976 that the illegal action had been staged by agents of the RCMP, helped by Montreal and Quebec provincial police.[53]

In mid-November 1972, the *Bulletin* announced its intention to change format: It would become a "popular bulletin" printed in large quantities. It took the opportunity to reflect upon its own evolution:

> We produce information by people committed to struggle. We produce critical, analytical information, the only way to provide readers with the means to think about reality. This information is not thought up in some office; it is created by establishing ties through political struggle and discussion with people in the information sector. . . . This information questions events, situations and groups in the overall relation of political forces in Quebec.[54]

The change of format was designed to broaden the appeal of militant information: "We will play our role as a committed press on a grander scale".[55]

At the same time, the APLQ addressed some friendly criticism to *Québec-Presse,* which it called the alternative to information consumerism. *Québec-Presse,* according to the APLQ, failed not only to distance itself from commercial media, but also tried to compete against them, often playing the same sensationalist game. Still, it was a voice of protest, attacking the system by exposing economic, electoral and governmental scandals. In the view of the APLQ, *Québec-Presse*'s work did help to weaken the current system, but something more was needed: "From its very foundation, the goal of the APLQ has been to remain in contact with grassroots groups involved in the struggle day after day. These groups will be the agents for change in Quebec."[56]

The APLQ opted for a dialectical relationship with its contributors, and would be linked neither to political parties nor to the unions in any direct way. The APLQ made it known that it was not in conflict with *Québec-Presse* or with the local media;

instead, its role was to break down the barriers of information, to drop profit-oriented commercialism in favour of clear writing about class relations.

In the issues that followed, the Agency made its involvement clear. In the last issue of 1972, it declared:

> In the context of the struggle for national liberation, it is important to see how situations evolve, and necessary to adapt our knowledge to them if we intend to triumph. We must follow the rhythm of objective changes in reality, avoid mistaking our dreams for reality and cutting ourselves off from it for the sake of activism or adventure. The commercial media are not about to reveal true power relations. The commercialism, sensationalism and ideology of these media are echoes of the voice of power.[57]

In the last five issues of the *Bulletin*, there was a sense that the APLQ was taking a more critical attitude towards some of the groups belonging to "what we broadly refer to as the popular movements". It seemed that the Agency was abandoning its role as a unifying force to take a stand in the debates, which were becoming ever more politicized and beginning to shake the movement during that period. The *Bulletin*'s last issue, number 117, came out at the end of June 1973. Issue 1 of the new *Bulletin populaire* would not appear until December. During that summer of transition, as militants made preparations for a new project, political positions hardened. This tension was typical of an emerging extreme left-wing discourse. In the autumn the APLQ team split. Those who held to the non-dogmatic approach found themselves in the minority and were forced to leave. Some of them were later to be involved in the launching of *Le Temps Fou* ("Crazy Time"), a "socialist, ecologist, feminist" review born in 1978.

The Agency was no longer a free information network, active throughout Quebec as the communication vehicle of new opposition movements. Its transformation was typical of the political changes in the air, changes in which communication issues would be foremost. The Agence de presse libre du Québec continued, but it had done its time.[58]

6. Union action: the media as catalyst

Along with the changes in the popular movement, the radicalization of the union movement at the beginning of the 1970s was one of the major developments in Quebec's social history. During this time the unions moved towards a total break with the dominant political and economic system.

At first this development was limited to rhetoric, but it wasn't long before labour groups joined together to create an inter-union Common Front. And in the fall of 1971 this new front received its baptism by fire. The occasion was a major conflict at the newspaper *La Presse,* which — as in 1964 — was once again the stage of an important repositioning of power in Quebec. In 1964, the information makers at the paper had demanded the right to cover current social changes; in 1971 they were part of those changes.

In 1971 each of the three big union centrals published a manifesto. In each case, they distanced themselves from the capitalist system and promised political action to replace capitalism by various forms of socialism.[59] In doing this they were breaking away from support for traditional political parties.

The union manifestos were among a number of recent analyses that had signalled the emergence of new ideologies. The Political Action Committees of the Montreal districts of Saint-Jacques and Maisonneuve — committees that had sprung from FRAP — had issued radical calls to action. New "popular movement support groups" such as the CFP, the CRIQ, the CCRPS and the Centre d'animation et de culture ouvrière (CACO — the "Workers' Cultural Centre") were similarly inspired by radical analysis and direction. Among social movements as a whole, there was greater hope for more systematic communication between groups, and a chance for more coherent and unified political action.[60] The CSN's manifesto was only the most succinct expression of the new mood. In it the writers "clearly state that Quebec does not have a future within the current economic system".[61] The manifesto was in many respects an economic and political successor to the *Parti pris* manifesto of 1965, although the latter tended to be seen as more of a cultural declaration.[62]

In its manifesto the CSN pointed to the path that unified organization might take. It incited members of the central to move towards political and ideological action, using popular information and participating, for instance, in the struggles of citizens' groups. The population as a whole had to be alerted to the break with traditional parties. It had to be made to "think collectively about possible solutions in a popular democratic regime". Workers must be encouraged to "undertake concrete struggles whose ultimate goal is to replace the current regime, dominated by the bourgeoisie, with a classless society — an economic system controlled by the workers".[63]

This renewal of ideological activity opened the door for militant trade unionism. Community groups and the union movements were on the same wavelength at this point and were prepared to react to capitalist offensives with new strategies. They were finally ready to take action to back up their words. In 1971, after a hot summer marked by legal and wildcat strikes throughout Quebec, an opportunity arose for common action involving all three union centrals and the popular groups.[64] A labour conflict broke out in the fall of 1971 at — where else? — *La Presse*.

As in 1964, the latest conflict at *La Presse* quickly took on monumental importance in the union movement. The unions realized this strike was one of those periodic battles that deeply transform union attitudes and practices.[65] On the surface, it was a case of technological change that would eliminate the jobs of several hundred printing-trade workers. In July 1971, *La Presse* locked out 321 pressmen, but the paper went on publishing. The pressmen did not set up picket lines, because, in spite of their desperate situation, they felt it was important for the newspaper to keep appearing. There are a half-dozen different unions at *La Presse* (both CSN and FTQ), and it soon became obvious that one of the owners' goals was to provoke a strike and confront their militancy once and for all.[66] Since the events of 1964, and especially since the rise of social unrest around 1968, relations between the owners and the CSN-affiliated journalists' union had been tense. During the winter of 1969-1970, the hardening conflict had set off a wildcat movement among journalists that ended with the occupation of the newsroom and the firing of one of the union leaders, Laval Le Borgne.[67]

In early October 1971, the journalists' union distributed a pamphlet entitled *Le dossier noir de l'information à* La Presse ("The Dark Side of the News at *La Presse*"), which termed the employer's actions in July "an anti-union offensive", and explained that the paper's journalists would rather continue their work than go out on strike.[68]

The *dossier noir* denounced the manipulation of the news, giving examples of what had occurred at *La Presse* since 1964. It cited numerous cases where unions were made to retreat, reducing journalists' power and increasing the owners' control of the news. There were concrete examples of censorship, truncated news stories, people having their jobs arbitrarily changed or simply eliminated.

Since financier Paul Desmarais had acquired *La Presse* in 1966, journalists, unions and all parties interested in the quality and freedom of information in Quebec had watched the paper's evolution with concern. People remembered how the coverage of the Saint-Jean-Baptiste Day riot in 1968 had been manipulated by upper-level management; they remembered the collusion with different levels of government during the October Crisis. Among progressive journalists, comments like this one — attributed to Paul Desmarais — raised concern: "I will not tolerate my journalists openly supporting the independence movement in *La Presse*."[69] In Quebec City, so it was said, upper-level civil servants were confident that a simple phone call to the news editor of *La Presse* was enough to remove a disturbing article from the front page and bury it back with the classifieds.[70] News had become a key sector in Quebec, and since it was also profitable, the stakes were higher than ever during the fall of 1971. And the marriage between big business and political power, incarnated by the owners of *La Presse,* was tighter than ever.[71]

The *La Presse* affair was seen as a sign of everything rotten in Quebec. The paper was a perfect target for the unions and the popular movement. As a result, a common front of the different unions at *La Presse*, bringing together workers from the FTQ and the CSN, called a massive solidarity demonstration for Friday evening, October 29. A few days before that rendez-vous, the *La Presse* owners ceased publication and closed their doors. Montreal's city fathers, always ready to accommodate the interests of big business, dusted off a three-year-old by-law forbidding demonstrations and, for the evening of the 29th, declared off-limits the area of the financial district where *La Presse* had its offices.

The demonstration went on anyway. More than fifteen thousand people turned out, making up the first large-scale, union-based demonstration in Quebec in recent times. For the first time manual and intellectual workers, students, activists from community groups and radical nationalists took to the streets together. (Only the Parti québécois was conspicuously absent.) What brought all these people together was a concern for information and its importance in the social struggle.

The newly awakened popular awareness of communication as an issue led people to look at its role in times of conflict. The nationalist, radical newsmagazine *Point de Mire* published an editorial in early December which concluded that the movement was poorly equipped for its task:

> What's obvious in the *La Presse* conflict and in labour struggles in general is how unions and popular movements, either for lack of funds or out of ignorance, tend not to use modern means of communication provided by the social sciences and technology. Yet these means are used on a day-to-day basis by their adversaries to crush them. Among other things, the conflict at *La Presse* reveals the archaic nature of the weapons used by unions in their battles. [72]

In fact, union action was relatively effective. A few days after the first demonstration, twelve thousand people turned out for a rally at the Montreal Forum. With CSN support, the journalists who had been laid off launched their own paper, the *Quotidien populaire* (literally, "People's Daily"). According to one participant, the paper was indeed to be "a true people's daily, a unique experience that would win the enthusiasm of everyone eager to see truth given its due. It will appeal to anyone who wants to see free information in Quebec." [73]

The *Quotidien populaire* published between sixty and eighty thousand copies and the unions finally had a way to show the public what free journalism was all about. The paper's large circulation was concrete proof of the movement's proportions and its influence on the population. For those directly involved, the experience of working without having to answer to a boss, without having to fit into a hierarchy, was not soon forgotten. Of course the *Quotidien populaire* could not go on without advertising or a distribution system. It lived to publish thirteen issues.[74]

The 1971 *La Presse* strike served as a catalyst for union solidarity in Quebec. But it was also a time when the aura of information was suddenly demystified, both by opposition social movements and information workers themselves. It was a unique moment when views on communication issues crystallized, and after which activists and journalists alike would be more aware of the ideological function of information.

7. May 1972: direct communication (2)

The *La Presse* conflict was the first common action undertaken by different strata of popular and union movements following the ideological radicalization of 1971. This kind of action was to continue in the months to come with the program of the inter-union Common Front of public sector workers. It was to reach its high point in the spring of 1972 with a wave of strikes that paralyzed much of Quebec society for several days.[75] These were the glory days of the protest movement of the time. And once again, the events helped along the development of unexpected innovations in the field of communications, bringing out new analyses, new strategies and a deeper awareness of the issues.

The role of the Employer-State had been expanding since the early 1960s, and as it grew, union action naturally came to be aimed at the State. According to some interpretations, the evolution of the union movement after 1967 was marked by a series of defensive responses to the political climate, despite the radical tone of union rhetoric.[76] This analysis would consider the Common Front of 1972 more like a tactical move than an element in an overall strategy. Yet dramatic action from the grassroots of the movement far outdistanced the directives coming from the union centrals, and toughened the conflict by bringing on a degree of militancy unthinkable up to then. The prevailing political mood seemed to foretell a break with the status quo.

In 1972 the collective agreements of all Quebec's provincial public and para-public employees including health-care workers and teachers were up for negotiation. For the first time, the three major union centrals involved — the CSN, FTQ and CEQ — were united in a Common Front. Their adversary was the government of Quebec.

At the start, the Common Front's strategy was established at a single table, where each central was represented.[77] This nerve centre was to handle all information addressed to the population at large, and was in charge of all attempts at widescale mobilization. But each central remained responsible for setting up its own internal support structure and for carrying out actions under the umbrella of the overall communication strategy.

The CSN and the CEQ tried to emphasize mobilization and information in their local activities. At the CSN this was translated into publishing brochures and special bulletins, or into sending out regular communications from the central to its members. However, when it came to talking to the population as a whole, the only available means for the Common Front were the mass media. As a result, the Common Front found itself in a classical dependency situation. As we might expect, the CSN's messages had a hard time getting through to the public without being totally distorted.

The CEQ's approach to the conflict was less directly political to begin with and its information network better tested. The CEQ was aware of the necessity of informing the public and of finding independent ways to do it. As a result it tried to augment its information tools but still maintain control over their conception and distribution. Its strategy included the traditional lobbying of a variety of established groups, parents' associations and other unions; participating in public meetings and similar events; distributing handbills and going door-to-door; the use of the mass media through press releases and paid advertising; infiltrating open-line radio shows and letters-to-the-editor columns in news-papers. Though there was nothing avant-garde about these tac-tics, they often meant the involvement of rank-and-file members. But, unfortunately, union members were often considered as nothing more than errand-runners carrying out a strategy con-ceived higher up — a strategy not necessarily any more sophis-ticated as a result.

As had been the case in other contexts in the past, union leaders seemed to ignore the problem of excessive dependence on traditional media, which could not be counted on to circulate counter-interpretations of social reality. Union strategists counted on the media's neutrality and ability to provide "honest reporting"; and banked on the support of a homogeneous public, provided the media coverage was "good".[78]

At the top, the 1972 Common Front brought with it few innovations. But the remarkable aspect of the conflict was the dramatic grassroots initiatives taken after negotiations broke down in May that year, and in spite of the hesitation of the union leadership. The result was the largest protest movement ever in modern Quebec (some would say, in North America), a move-ment involving more than three hundred thousand workers. Among other things, when the chips were down ideas and new types of action came from far-flung regions, contrary to the myth that radical politics is a big-city phenomenon. And once again, one of the main ingredients of the movement took the form of direct communication carried out by the people involved.

In the spring of 1972, public sector negotiations bogged down, while the Common Front tried to speed them up by exerting pressure.[79] In March and April, teachers went out on a series of wildcat strikes before being forced back to their jobs by emergency legislation. In the union locals, workers were losing patience with the sluggishness of their leaders' strategy.

In the mass media the climate was one of anti-union hysteria. Media coverage of the conflicts did not fail to provoke some groups of workers: On April 17, in Rivière-du-Loup, workers occupied the local radio station — a sign of things to come.

As part of its information campaign, the Common Front had prepared a series of TV shows. On Monday, May 2, Channel 10 in Montreal (part of the privately-owned network Télé-Métropole) refused to broadcast a scheduled show paid for by the Common Front. Ten days later, the Common Front would not have to pay to use the station's antenna. . . .

In early May wildcat strikes became more widespread and spilled over into the private sector as well. Along the North Shore and in other highly industrialized and unionized regions, normal activities were suspended as whole cities were occupied by workers: Sept-Îles, Baie-Comeau, Port-Cartier and Hauterive on the North Shore, Murdochville in the Gaspé, Chibougamau on the way to James Bay and Thetford Mines in the asbestos region. In each of these cities and towns, commando groups of workers spontaneously took over radio and, in some cases, television stations. Regular programming was pre-empted by union news and "political, revolutionary" music.

The tactic was repeated between May 10 and 14, especially on May 12, the day of the general strike throughout Quebec. For varying amounts of time over these few days, workers controlled TV or radio stations in Saint-Jérôme, Sherbrooke, Joliette, Sorel, Lévis, Amos, Rouyn-Noranda, Rimouski, Beauceville, Ville-Marie, Matane and New Carlisle, as well as in Chicoutimi, Quebec City and Montreal. In the Montreal area, radio stations CKLM, CKVL and CFGL were occupied, while demonstrations took place in front of CKAC and CJMS. In addition, the six Montreal dailies did not publish on May 12, after a delegation of workers from La Presse visited all the newsrooms. At Radio-Canada, the technicians' union (NABET) went out, paralyzing the network in Montreal, Quebec City and Chicoutimi. In Saint-Jérôme in the Laurentians, the weekly paper L'Echo du Nord was out of action as well. And on the 12th of May, the Common Front-sponsored program that had been banished from Télé-Métropole ten days earlier was broadcast province-wide on the network's eight stations.

An interesting sidelight occurred during the night of May 13-14 when a group of Common Front militants visited the

Québec-Presse printing plant while the paper was being put together. The Common Front had already agreed to let *Québec-Presse* publish on a regular basis, because it was the only paper dedicated to workers' interests. The visit, apparently, was the result of a local initiative to check the paper's content. As a protest against the Parti québécois' position on the Common Front, the workers demanded the withdrawal of a column by PQ executive member Jacques Parizeau. The delegation took over the space reserved for Parizeau and used it to publish its own statement, which it headed "May there be two, three, many Sept-Îles", a reference to the North-Shore town under worker occupation. Among the delegation were members of the Agence de presse libre du Québec. As they explained later, they had come to show their support for *Québec-Presse* journalists, who did not appreciate the visit at all.

This incident illustrates the complexities that were developing in protest movements over the communication question; on the whole, the Common Front was a good example of this. The direct take-over of information media during the 1972 general strike gave workers a feeling of what it was like to assume control of the means of production of public opinion, and to create independent means of informing the population. The unionists carried this out in the same spirit of unity, grassroots action and self-management that characterized the strike movement. Traditional information channels were caught in their own trap, as they had been during the October Crisis of 1970. Just by covering the workers' dramatic moves — which they could not keep themselves from doing — the media fuelled the fire, contributing — albeit involuntarily — to the movement's momentum. At this extraordinary moment, communication and social action shared a common thrust.

MIXED MESSAGES: THE 1970s

4

The 1972 general strike marked an end to the turbulent period that Quebec society had experienced since 1967-68. By 1973 the opposition movements, which in preceding years had strengthened their position, began to splinter. Before, even though no one could claim that perfect unity reigned everywhere, there was at least a sense of solidarity ranged against an identifiable adversary: the alliance of capital and the State. From 1973 onward, however, movements for social and political change became more and more divergent and often defined themselves in opposition to one another.

Political movements, as we shall see, usually took one of two approaches in their relationship to media. The first, which its advocates called the revolutionary approach, was distinguished by the use of propaganda methods without any effective link to a corresponding social practice. The second, reformist in nature — because it was oriented towards a more immediate political objective — was distinguished by an almost complete absence of conscious communication strategy tailored to its own needs. Both these choices led to political dead ends and in the early 1980s activists were still trying to find a way out of the impasse.

1. Popular and union movements at the crossroads
The euphoria that followed the May 1972 general strike soon dissipated, to be followed by hard times for the opposition move-

ments. On the union front, the May militancy created a split within the Confédération des syndicats nationaux (CSN), as a conservative wing that had organized in reaction to the central's 1971 manifesto began to stir. In 1972-73, the split finally resulted in the departure of forty thousand unionized private-sector workers from the CSN, most of them led by three dissident leaders who then formed the Centrale des syndicats démocratiques (CSD — Organization of Democratic Unions).

A similar mood of political retrenchment settled over the other union centrals, where "moderate" elements were soon elected to executive positions. In the Centrale de l'enseignement du Québec (CEQ), for example, left-wing activists who had spearheaded the ideological activities of the early 1970s were banished from the upper-level posts they had held within the central.[1]

The mainstream media, by their very nature, contributed to the weakening of the left. The media took it upon themselves to interpret the often abstruse positions and strident declarations of union "radicals". In many cases, media reports were the only way rank-and-file members could learn what their own democratic institutions were doing. The "radicals" thus became sitting ducks for the less progressive elements who were looking to recapture lost ground. For instance, by supporting the faction opposed to the radicalization of the CSN, the media objectively contributed to the union's split and the creation of the CSD.[2]

In general, the union movement of the time wavered between solidarity and division. The split within the CSN was followed by a unified, inter-union movement for the liberation of the presidents of the three union centrals — Marcel Pépin, Louis Laberge and Yvon Charbonneau — who had been imprisoned for violating back-to-work legislation in the May 1972 strike. In 1973, the old labour tradition of celebrating May Day was revived, and major demonstrations took place across Quebec. Yet a short time after that, sharp divisions returned to haunt the unions in the wake of the revelations of the government Commission of Inquiry into the Construction Industry (the Cliche Commission), which set up a rivalry between unions within the FTQ and the

CSN. In 1974, these deep fissures rendered the centrals powerless to maintain their material support for *Québec-Presse*.[3]

On the other hand, the union movement displayed a certain maturity. Especially among younger unionized workers and activists, several years of continuous conflict had begun to create a new culture, a sense of solidarity and a feeling of belonging to a common entity. Whether we call this new disposition "the working class" or not, it made a definitive mark on the social scene. From then on, there was a section — small but still important — of society that would see itself as united against established political and economic authority, and influenced by a social awareness of domination and exploitation. The publication of union newspapers and local bulletins, controlled by the grass-roots, was a sign of that awareness. Such publications came to be considered necessary tools for any union engaged in militant action.[4] They were also the expression of a type of political unionism that was trying to use information as part of its arsenal.

As in the case of the unionists, it is necessary to go back to 1971 to trace the ideological radicalization of the popular groups. Beginning in that year a number of political action committees, formerly affiliated with FRAP, tried to work out a more radical theoretical approach to politics, and to translate this shift into action.

In 1971, members of the Saint-Jacques Comité d'action politique (CAP — Political Action Committee) reactivated the review *Mobilisation,* "a review for militants, by militants". The publication had been abandoned in 1970 after the FLP disbanded (see chapter 2.2). At first it was not a theoretical review, but rather an analytical one examining various contemporary conflicts (unemployment, education in political committees, the fight against the East-West Montreal expressway, the OFY projects). In the fourth issue of the new series, the Saint-Jacques committee published a major political text that sent shockwaves through the Quebec left: *Bâtir une organisation politique des travailleurs québécois* ("Building a Political Organization of Quebec Workers").[5] This text, written in the wake of the October

Crisis, updated some older theoretical texts, including the 1965 *Parti pris* manifesto. The Saint-Jacques committee concluded that the October Crisis showed the FLQ's style of action did lead to a certain awareness, but lacked lasting results. For popular discontent to be durable and instrumental, Quebec needed "an autonomous working-class political organization".

This was the start of a debate that would absorb the energies of opposition movements for the greater part of the 1970s. In April 1972, members of the Maisonneuve Political Action Committee also rallied around *Mobilisation*. The Saint-Jacques and Maisonneuve committees announced that they were leaving FRAP and starting instead to work towards a political organization of the working class. They intended to evaluate the successes and failures of past propaganda efforts and to engage in action-research into better ways to reach "the masses". For a time, these militants practised a policy of "implantation", which meant getting jobs in factories in working-class neighbourhoods, researching living and working conditions among the "labouring classes" and developing tools for education and information. After the sixth issue, *Mobilisation* suspended publication, but the transformation of the popular movement to which it had contributed was irreversible.

At the same time the political climate of the left was characterized by arguments over strategy and theory that may have determined future political action but also tended to isolate the movement from its political base.[6] Typical of this discussion was an exchange of polemic between two old hands who had been in the Quebec left since the days of *Révolution québécoise:* Pierre Vallières and Charles Gagnon. Though they had both been accused (and acquitted) of the charge of "seditious conspiracy" during the October Crisis, Vallières and Gagnon had parted ways. Vallières had chosen to give critical support to the Parti québécois and priority to political independence (a position he was to abandon once and for all several years later after the PQ took power). Gagnon proposed dismissing the national question and concentrating on creating a "proletarian party".[7] Gagnon's positions, contained in a 1972 pamphlet entitled *Pour le parti prolétarien,* ("Towards the Proletarian Party") led to the creation in 1973 of the Marxist-Leninist group En lutte! (In Struggle) and the newspaper of the same name.

This new line contained one fundamental difficulty: The entire tradition of opposition social movements in Quebec since 1960 had been characterized by a belief in the ability of people to organize themselves by appropriating the necessary powers, and *not* through a dominating, structured party. There had been no previous indications that the "masses" concerned by this kind of action would want anything to do with a centralized authoritarian political structure. Marxist-Leninist militants used experiences like May 1972 to discredit union leadership, pointing out that the leaders had been by-passed by events. But they did not seem to realize that the radical actions of 1972 were based on a series of free and spontaneous initiatives absolutely incompatible with a centralized, highly-disciplined political apparatus.

From 1973 on, the formation of the Political Action Committees and Marxist-Leninist groups brought some basic changes to Quebec opposition movements. First of all, the new groupings constituted a theoretical break characterized by the increasing influence of orthodox Marxism. In addition, these groups introduced a new kind of political involvement that emphasized the process of organizing workers according to strategic principles worked out by Lenin in Europe at the turn of the century. This political phenomenon and the climate it created would dominate opposition movements for several years, and would remain beyond the comprehension of many activists until well into the 1980s.[8] Far from being immune to it, the communications area was probably one of the most affected by it.

2. Militancy and propaganda: Bulletin populaire and Mobilisation

The more radical political positions within the popular movement brought with them new forms of communication — or rather, modifications in communication. Popular movement support groups — groups whose activity was in the ideological arena — continued to proliferate and define their actions in relation to the eventual establishment of a workers' party. Groups involved in the field of communications, like the Agence de presse libre du Québec, started to see what they were doing as making propaganda, subordinating ideological work to political organizing. However, unlike *Parti pris,* for example, which had been a force for cultural unity despite its failed political pretensions, publications such as the *Bulletin populaire* and *Mobilisation* fragmented the movement and caused the disappearance of several useful and important groups.

We pick up the trail of the APLQ in the wake of its decision to launch a wide-circulation current affairs magazine. In December 1973, the APLQ's *Bulletin populaire* began publication as a bimonthly magazine, some thirty pages long and selling for fifty cents a copy. Unlike the APLQ's former *Bulletin,* the new production could be bought on the newsstands. It was printed on presses the APLQ had purchased thanks to loans from a variety of student and union organizations. The *Bulletin populaire* reached a peak sale of some two thousand copies, with seven hundred subscribers.

The *Bulletin populaire* was designed to be a "tool of struggle for those suffocating in the straightjacket of the capitalist system, for those protesting against the authority of the big bosses".

> [The] *Bulletin populaire* is designed to help explain how capitalism functions, what its crises are, how it contributes to individual and collective degradation. It intends to present the beginnings of a workers' organization in Quebec, learning from international revolutionary struggles and efforts to build socialism.[9]

This manifesto reveals an orientation similar to that of the 1971-72 version of *Mobilisation.* In fact, organic links had begun to form between the two groups; the *Bulletin populaire* was produced by the APLQ which, since January 1973, belonged to a collective which had decided once again to relaunch the review *Mobilisation.* Other groups in the collective were the Political Action Committees from Saint-Jacques, Maisonneuve, Côte des Neiges and Pointe Saint-Charles (all Montreal neighbourhoods).

The destiny of these two enterprises — the *Bulletin populaire*, produced as a tool of support for popular struggles and aimed at a wide audience, and *Mobilisation*, limited to a small circle of politically active militants — was closely joined between 1973 and 1976, and the paths they took spoke eloquently of the evolution of the popular movement over those years.

These two publishing projects were distinguished by an almost constant effort to define and redefine objectives, means and self-images. The members expended a great deal of energy on clarifying their political line and the role they should play — a search for identity clearly apparent in the many criticisms and self-criticisms the two reviews published.

From the very beginning, the *Bulletin populaire* set out to distinguish itself from the old APLQ *Bulletin*. The APLQ had wanted to "fight censorship, construct an information network free from the limitations of the bourgeois press, point out exploit-ation and alienation and be a witness to the development of progressive forces at work in a variety of struggles."[10] Designed to be a "parallel" press agency, the APLQ had been underused, said the *Bulletin populaire*, because its subscriptions cost too much and its potential membership (the militant press) was too small. The *Bulletin populaire* team concluded that a wide-distribution paper would be better designed for the groups it wanted to reach.

"Today," they continued, "the APLQ defines itself as an ideological group." But the *Bulletin populaire* was not just an improved version of the old bulletin: "It represents a step forward in the clarification of our political orientation and our informa-tion policy."[11]

The *Bulletin populaire* took on a newsmagazine format. It provided counter-information on subjects such as local union conflicts, working and living conditions in various neighbour-hoods and counter-culture events, using language richer in social distinctions than that usually employed by the mainstream media. It also chose to cover concrete conflicts in much greater depth than traditional media. To celebrate the third anniversary of the APLQ, the *Bulletin populaire* stated: "By increasing links with progressive groups and socialist militants, the APLQ team can count on a better developed political base and be a more effective tool directly serving the objective of building the working class's political organization."[12]

It is possible to follow the political evolution of the magazine issue by issue because each one usually included a small editor's note. For instance, on June 13, 1974, the *Bulletin populaire* declared it would go further than the APLQ's former bulletin in both information and analysis. The former bulletin had been oriented towards "all popular and workers' struggles", while the new version would concentrate on "the independent organization of the working class". This change was supposed to be better adapted to presenting events from a working-class perspective. The magazine would analyze the way current conflicts were being handled, would discuss the general political situation and political initiatives. But it could be argued that this approach actually represented a narrowing of influence and interest, because it was limited to highly-committed activists, and that it fed the emerging power struggles between political sub-groups within this small circle.[13]

This problem was even more apparent in issues of the magazine *Mobilisation* published during the same period. The groups involved in putting out the magazine were the Saint-Jacques and Maisonneuve Political Action Committees, the left-wing bookstore Librairie progressiste and the APLQ. Aimed exclusively at militants, *Mobilisation* more openly attacked the major political questions of the day, and took a more determined position on the points of view of other groups. The review concentrated its energies on current conflicts and political activities, as well as on theoretical and strategic issues: political education, the study of Marxism, the applications of Marxist analysis. At the beginning the effort seemed to be an attempt to create understanding among militant groups, to unify them. But as time went by, it became an attempt to impose political hegemony.

In its June 1973 issue, *Mobilisation* launched a debate on propaganda, and invited interested parties to participate, including the APLQ, the publishers of *En lutte!* and Librairie progress-iste. The main issue: Does propaganda have an independent role or should it be linked to political organization?[14]

Mobilisation summed up what had been done in the prop-aganda field in Quebec over the last ten years. It considered *Parti pris*/Mouvement de libération populaire as a first step in linking ideological practice to the building of a revolutionary party, as an experience that had influenced progressive intellectu-als without really developing a large-scale propaganda instru-ment for the working class. The Front de libération populaire, according to *Mobilisation,* took things a step further by practis-ing mass propaganda in its paper *La Masse,* with its militant review, its various wildcat activities involving handbill distribu-tion, spray-painting, the use of political stickers and wall-postering, its public debates, rallies and demonstrations. The FLP, however, limited itself to agit-prop without developing any organizational alternatives. The FLQ experience in 1970 and the downfall of FRAP showed that it was necessary to redefine politi-cal orientations whereas a group like the APLQ had always preached a relative independence from the ideological arena.

Mobilisation seemed to be opting for a marriage between political and ideological priorities, subordinating the ideological to strategic considerations. The review was reorganized in the fall of 1973, and it took the opportunity to put forward this new position.[15] From then on, the editors declared, *Mobilisation* would be "a means of exchange and education whose goal will be to clarify the ideological and political orientation of those groups working towards building a proletarian party". However, the magazine was still quite different from the work of a group like En lutte!, which insisted that the organizational aspects of the new party had to be Marxist-Leninist — that is, centralized, disci-plined and with a strict hierarchy.

The debate continued along these lines and influenced politi-cal movements through publications like the *Bulletin populaire, Mobilisation, En lutte!* and other more local initiatives. The size of the movement involved in this power struggle can be gauged by the number of local publications coming from community groups and union militants. In the fall of 1972, not less than twenty-four periodicals of this type were distributed in the Montreal region alone. In 1975 the number of union publications alone stood at twenty.[16]

Either partially or completely, every group was forced to speak to the question of political organization and, more specifically, of building the party. During this time (1973-74), although groups whose main concern was ideological work[17] were more deeply involved in this debate, even tenants' associations, food co-ops, daycare centres, groups of welfare recipients, consumers' groups — not to mention union centrals — had to respond to the basic question raised by the "M-Ls".[18]

This Marxist-Leninist emphasis on party building became clear enough in the various tactical manoeuvres of the time. For example, in the fall of 1974 there was talk in Montreal of making a new attempt to channel popular urban movements towards municipal politics. A new group, the Montreal Citizens' Movement (MCM), was launched to participate in the city elections. The MCM did not have the organic links with popular and union movements that FRAP did in 1970, but circumstances were different. In fact, the MCM came into being thanks to a common effort by the Comité régional intersyndical de Montréal (CRIM — Inter-Union Regional Committee of Montreal), the Montreal-Centre region of the Parti québécois and by veterans of various urban community struggles in the city over the years. Had the MCM been born several years earlier, it would certainly have enjoyed the support of the broader social movements from which it had sprung. But in the context of the time, the more "advanced" sectors — that is, those close to the Marxist-Leninist current — disowned it. Both the *Bulletin populaire* and *Mobilisation* took harsh attitudes toward the MCM.[19]

3. Self-criticism, redefinitions — and liquidation

Debating, clarifying one's orientation, honing the correct line — all continued apace. In October 1974, *Mobilisation* revealed the debate that was raging between two tendencies within the magazine.[20] The Librairie progressiste and the Centre de recherche et d'information sur le Québec (CRIQ) continued putting out the magazine, while the APLQ and the Political Action Committees opted out. The subsequent issues of the *Bulletin populaire* and *Mobilisation* were filled with the most arcane details of the latest political developments, which quickly took over the space usually reserved for other matters.

Mobilisation's final 1974 issue was concerned solely with ideological work.[21] This task, which consisted in giving a clear "class" character to whatever action was undertaken, involved an arduous struggle over questions of style and presentation. The magazine admitted the revolutionaries had often been unable to make the masses understand their ideas, and stressed that neighbourhood newspapers and factory broadsheets were important means of communication. In the same issue, the Librairie progressiste team, in a signed article, pointed out that ideological work could take on different forms depending on the times: For example, a party newspaper could unify various local groups around a specific strategy if it used propaganda as a way of creating unity. They gave the example of *Iskra,* the Bolshevik paper founded by Lenin around 1900 to promote his party among the militant groups of the time.

During this period, the *Bulletin populaire* was also redefining its purpose. In its last 1974 issue it declared that "the principal objective of the team is to work on the founding of a working-class political organization to overthrow capitalism in Quebec".[22] The APLQ, it seemed, was to have another vocation besides informing people, no matter how radical its information. What stood between the APLQ and *Mobilisation* was the issue of the relationship of the party to popular organizations, an issue that might appear abstract and shrouded in darkness for the uninitiated, but one that was of great importance at the time. Should the more politicized members impose their "advanced" knowledge on the groups they were involved in, or should they stand back and wait for the masses to advance to their level?

On March 6, 1975, the *Bulletin populaire* "clarified its orientation". It would work towards the creation of a working-class political organization whose goal was to build socialism.

In the current state of affairs, with the totality of information being controlled by spokesmen for the bourgeoisie, the *Bulletin* is a way of presenting a class point of view on the major events determining society's direction. This task of propaganda on working-class issues presents concrete conditions for building a tool for information, analysis and education to forward the workers' struggles against the bourgeoisie and to contribute towards building a political organization. In this way, the *Bulletin* is not only an alternative to the bourgeois press, but most of all the starting point of a socialist press within the working class.[23]

Could this have been a momentary regression towards idealizing the potential role of information as an agent of social change? Not really, since the authors still insisted on a type of information that tied in with political analysis and strategy. The two main lines for future action were to demonstrate how the cultural, social, economic and political situation "primarily depends on the imperialist domination of the American bourgeoisie in Quebec"; and to "use concrete examples to show how working-class strength may better be built in Quebec".

The *Bulletin populaire* would agree to work only with certain groups, those "who recognized the priority of building a socialist political organization". The *Bulletin* would go beyond the role of informing and analyzing "to develop organizational perspectives from successful experiences elsewhere". In its own words, the paper would become "a lifeline between various groups active among the working class". Its informational work thus became an aspect of organizational activity — given, for example, the selection it made between groups it would support, those it would ignore and those it would denounce. By making these choices it imitated one of the most basic characteristics of the bourgeois press: It made a seemingly neutral press serve an ideology and a political strategy.

A few issues later, the *Bulletin populaire* published a political text entitled *Construisons notre force* ("Let's Build Our Strength") in which it again clarified the wider objectives of the movement to which it belonged.[24] The party's organization was presented as the solution to a variety of persistent social evils which would lead to wide-ranging social change. The group declared that its agit-prop work was limited, modest and isolated in the absence of a political organization. The only work worth undertaking was action which would hasten the founding of such an organization.

In the summer of 1975, in a spirit of consolidation, *Mobilisation* published the record of its two first years.[25] It reminded the readers that the magazine had been reorganized in the fall of 1973 "to become a means of continual reflection and clarification for militants". It had acted as a political organ for the revolutionary movement in the widest sense of the term (following the tradition of the FLP in 1969-70 and the Political Action Committees in 1971-72). It had survived the schisms of fall 1974 to become the organ of a tendency within the new revolutionary Marxist-Leninist movement. It owned up to the fact that this movement was much more limited than a number of broader social movements and that, furthermore, the revolutionary wing was itself splintered into different political factions.

In this article, *Mobilisation* labelled the APLQ as "reformist". The APLQ's *Bulletin populaire* text *Construisons notre force,* which had tried to take a position between the open reformism of many of the groups of the time and the revolutionary Marxist-Leninist orientation, earned the comment that the APLQ was guilty of "petty-bourgeois hesitation", like so many other reform groups.

From September 1975 onward, *Mobilisation* defined itself as a "Marxist-Leninist review appearing monthly".[26] It didn't need to define its goals any further; the label spoke for itself. With the September issue, *Mobilisation* also announced its intention to become a Marxist-Leninist organization. It declared that the Quebec revolutionary movement had emerged from its childhood (1965-74), and finished its adolescence (1974-75), to arrive at "the moment of truth". Now as the organ of a specific current, the magazine would no longer be a "universal loud-speaker for the left". No longer would it be produced by a "heterogeneous collective" (especially since CRIQ had pulled out). A unified political team "responsible to the organization that we are building" would be the publisher.

Then, mysteriously, no more was heard from *Mobilisation* until April 15, 1976, when the group published its self-criticism in a pamphlet called *Liquidons le spontanéisme, l'opportunisme, et l'économisme* (Let's Liquidate Spontaneism, Opportunism and Economism"). This text, which has since become a classic of the Quebec far-left, declared that *Mobilisation* had represented "the right-wing opportunist line in the revolutionary movement", and that finally "a rectification movement" had taken over the review to liquidate it once and for all.[27]

So began the wave of "liquidations" that would destroy several of the most active groups in the years that followed. Fortunately, not all attempts at liquidation succeeded, and efforts to stop the activities of some groups or to integrate them into Marxist-Leninist orthodoxy were defeated by members and popular support. But almost all major groups were forced to confront attempts at liquidation.

The point of the liquidation movement, rather mystifying in itself, was to correct past errors, especially the sin of having believed that the revolutionary party could be built "from within the masses", that is, according to popular will. In its self-criticism, *Mobilisation* quoted Lenin: "In his work [*What Is To Be Done?*], he totally demolishes the spontaneist thesis of building the party from below and scientifically proves that the only proper way to build the proletarian party is to do so from the top down."[28]

This approach was in total contradiction to the spirit behind Quebec opposition movements since 1960. But it did hold a strong attraction for militants seeking absolute answers and the direct route towards the revolution. More often than not, it would wreak confusion within groups whose members had been working sincerely over the years to create effective action on the basis of democratic self-management.

The liquidation movement affected, among others, the community media. Paradoxically, the least reform-minded media were most quickly convinced to abandon their work and rally behind a political group. The Conseil de développement des média communautaires (Community Media Development

Council), created in 1973, self-destructed under the guise of liquidation in January of 1977.[29] Other notable liquidations in the cultural area: CRIQ, the review *Stratégies,* the Centre d'animation culturelle ouvrière (Workers' Cultural Centre), the Comité d'information politique (Political Information Committee) and the Librairie progressiste. Among those who rejected liquidation attempts was the Centre de formation populaire, still active and independent well into the 1980s.[30]

One of the victims of the liquidationist tide was the *Bulletin populaire.* Over the summer and fall of 1975, the team continued defining and redefining its orientation, a process that readers could follow through subtle changes in the editor's short note beginning every issue. At the end of the year, the review entered a new period of clarification. The first issue of 1976 revealed: "Our current objective is to build a working-class political party, guided by the revolutionary science of the proletariat: Marxism-Leninism." And later: "The main concern of the APLQ is to join in developing a correct political line. This is why we publish the *Bulletin populaire.*"[31]

A few issues later the APLQ engaged in self-criticism, admitting to having overestimated the importance of propaganda — a fact attributed to the "petty-bourgeois origins and situation" of the members of the team.[32] They said they had been unable to master Marxist-Leninist historical teachings, and had idealized the working class. The remedy? Reduce the review from thirty-two to twenty pages: "This reduction is part of the clarification process. Reducing the number of pages will lead to better conditions for debate and study."

The following issue included a letter from a former collaborator who insisted that the APLQ break with its past: "The current ideological shift toward M-L positions suggests that there is no qualitative break between the worker/populist positions of the old agency and the movement."[33] The correspondent wanted the APLQ to choose: either disappear and have its individual members rally to M-L groups, or transform itself from an agency into a political Marxist-Leninist organization.

The team responded: "The agency's members are currently working on political clarification and there is no doubt that this will lead to a break with our past action."[34] But the *Bulletin populaire* published a final issue, its fifty-ninth, without saying a word about the conclusion to this political debate.

This rather bizarre chain of events would have been amusing if it hadn't been so disastrous. In fact, the M-L tendency, most strongly represented by En Lutte!, founded in 1973, and by the Canadian Communist League (Marxist-Leninist), founded in 1975 and transformed into the Workers' Communist Party in 1979, caused a lot of trouble within social movements in 1975-76. It was able to liquidate or subjugate a whole series of ideological groups and carve itself a monopoly in this area. Its actions were so widely felt that even in the 1980s several sectors of the community and workers' movements are still ideologically dominated by the vestiges of the M-L current.[35]

But what interests us here is the idea of information as propaganda, and the relation between this idea and political action. Is communication merely an instrument in political action? Or must it be an integral, organic part of such action? This is the question raised by the experiences we have looked at; we will return to it in our conclusion. But before that, we will consider some totally different pathways.

4. What the media make, the media shall unmake: the Montreal Citizen's Movement

Despite the strong influence of Marxist-Leninists, their tendency was not the only one, or even the dominant one, during the 1970s. Quite the opposite; in the middle of the decade new types of political involvement had taken hold in Quebec society. The new movements were particularly concerned with the quality of social life: women's rights, ecological matters, urban issues and sexual issues joined the more classical questions related to the workplace. There was a feeling of a fresh departure, especially since the promoters of these movements often gave the impression that they knew nothing of what had gone on in the preceding years. Strategically, they often appeared naive and idealistic,

especially as far as communication was concerned. They sometimes created small independent publications for themselves, but
often produced no more than simple handbills that circulated a
few rudimentary ideas among a limited number of readers. Or
worse, they did not establish their own channels of communication and depended exclusively on mainstream media to "get their
message across". Politically, however, these movements represented an important step away from the Marxist-Leninist limitations, and they were often rewarded with success. Their communication practices are worth examining closely, and we will
start with one particular case: the Montreal Citizens' Movement
(MCM).[36]

The MCM was created in 1974 with the immediate goal of
entering the city elections scheduled for that fall. In a certain
sense the successor to FRAP, the MCM represented a much larger
undertaking. Its launching involved a variety of groups, including regional associations of the Parti québécois; the CRIM (Inter-
Union Regional Committee), which represented the three main
union centrals; the Quebec wing of the New Democratic Party;
and non-aligned militants from a host of urban groups. Members
of various community associations also got on the bandwagon, as
well as newcomers cutting their teeth on political action.

Naturally, the political climate of the times had a great influence on the MCM's beginnings. Appearing on the political scene
at a time when urban decay was at its worse, the MCM attracted
more liberal than revolutionary minds. It was also courted by the
mass media which, hot on the Watergate trail, decided that
municipal politics in Montreal was only slightly less scandalous.
These circumstances gave the MCM the appearance of a broad
base, but deprived it of the active support of much of the dynamic
base of the old FRAP group, which included the most radical
elements of union and popular movements. The MCM also drew
flack from the Marxist-Leninist movement which rejected anything that was not organized with a view towards the eventual
"party".

Very early on the MCM distinguished itself by heated internal
debates, often centred around terminology. One of the first

points under discussion concerned the MCM's target clientele. The group finally decided that it would address itself to "citizens" and not to "workers", a move that alienated certain union supporters but gave increased access to the media. It spent much time debating the structure of the party — for by now it was clear that a "party" was being created — and decided finally to organize along geographical electoral districts, which would allow any "citizen" to join. This decision eliminated the possibility of organic links with popular and union movements, which is what FRAP had aimed for, and what popular and union groups would have wanted.

But on the other hand, the political mood of 1974 favoured the new party and soon translated into tangible popular support. On election day the incumbent Civic Party of Montreal had still not taken the opposition very seriously, and its lethargy helped elect eighteen MCM councillors (out of fifty-five seats) with 44 per cent of the vote.

The MCM's platform favoured the working class and used populist language. But, because its platform could be interpreted in any of several directions, there was plenty of room for ambiguity. After the election, the MCM found itself pulled in three directions at once. One grouping — which came to be called the "radical" or "socialist" wing — supported extra-parliamentary action. Another (the "moderates" or "social-democrats") put emphasis on parliamentary action; and a third, rather unsure of what it thought, would accept radical action as long as it was sufficiently prettified to appeal to the public at large (and, just as important, to the mainstream media, which was seen as the main channel between the party and the people).

For example, soon after the MCM's arrival at City Hall, its councillors presented a motion calling for free public transport for senior citizens (one of its campaign promises — in fact, the MCM program called for free public transport across the board). The administration of the city's transport system responded by announcing a schedule of reduced fares for seniors — clearly a moral victory for the opposition. When the time came to vote on the administration's proposal at City Hall, the MCM's general council instructed its representatives to vote against the proposal, as a way of keeping its more radical position in public view. Moderates in the party were outraged at this decision, which they feared would be misinterpreted by the public, and in City Council every MCM member but one finally voted with the administration. The incident showed all the difficulties of combining parliamentary and extra-parliamentary politics, and set the tone of the party's internal relations for years to come.

The tension among the MCM's internal tendencies was exacerbated by the fact that the radicals were stronger in party structures, while the moderates dominated the councillors' caucus. The populist centre comprised much of the general membership.

Tensions increased within the MCM when it became apparent that the newly-elected councillors enjoyed privileged status because of their easy access to the mass media. As far as the media were concerned, the elected councillors were the official spokesmen of the MCM — even if that went against party practice, which treated the elected members as delegates rather than representatives. But political reality soon made it impossible for the democratic structures of the party (executive, general council, convention, district general assemblies) to "control" the elected members. In effect, the councillors possessed a double mandate, both as "duly elected representatives of the people", and as representatives of a party committed to internal democracy. Given the prevailing political culture of the society, it was much more natural for them to define themselves in relation to the public rather than the party.

Meanwhile the media, in their quest for "news", and with their tendency to gravitate towards description and away from analysis, concentrated on the official spokespersons instead of examining what was going on at the base. The media were to play an important role in the internal dynamics of the MCM.

When the party's internal tensions were played out in public via debates inside the various party structures, the media took it as a sign of weakness. Editorial writers worried about splits and signs of lack of unity within the party. Certain high-profile figures within the MCM, skillful at manipulating the media, took advantage of their media access to take the debate outside the party and appeal to public opinion. Curiously enough, that did not really work. The moderates were unable to take over the party apparatus controlled by the radicals with the support of the populists. Yet the moderates controlled the MCM's public image by mastering relations with the media, and so it was their minority interpretation of what the party was about that was media-certified as the legitimate one.

In the fall of 1976, the situation came to a head. The two main tendencies were preparing for the annual convention, each with the goal of digging in once and for all and outflanking the other. Typically, the left wing beforehand went into a long period of collectively examining the situation, followed by the arduous writing of a new platform that would clarify its radical orientation. The moderates did their campaigning essentially in the mainstream media. The left, for example, proposed a new chapter to the MCM program, one that would spell out the form to be taken by the democratic neighbourhood councils an MCM administration would help create. The right denounced the proposed structures as "soviets" and needless to say, that's what made the headlines. The final decision, however, was up to party members, not the public at large: The left won the convention but the MCM's popular stock dropped considerably.

At the time, the MCM was totally dependent on mainstream media to reach the population. Unlike the union movement, for example, the MCM had never developed any independent means of communication, no matter how primitive. In addition, with the far left hostility to the party, it could not count on the support of publications like the *Bulletin populaire* or *Mobilisation;* those organs had already denounced the party. *Québec-Presse* was a thing of the past: Ironically, its final issue came out the day the MCM made its triumphant entry into City Hall. The pro-independence daily *Le Jour* began casting a critical eye on the party once the internal debates started heating up. And in any case, this paper, too, went out of existence in the summer of 1976. The MCM had never kept its distance from mainstream media in the days when media approval benefited it, and as a result the party was totally at their mercy when the media finally changed their minds.

At this point, the MCM should have realized it was time to rethink its method of operation. A communication strategy would have to be designed. The party could no longer count on the support of the media alone to widen its base, yet it could not ignore them as long as its political goals required reaching large parts of the population. It had few resources at its disposal in the "alternative" media, and none to speak of under its own control.

The way out of this dilemma was not easy, but the problem was never really a top priority for party strategists. They continued searching for "good coverage" from the media and often organized party action with this in mind without ever really dealing with the need to establish a more direct and organic relation to their constituency.

When the time came for the 1978 municipal elections, the jig was up. A third party had been set up for the occasion, a tidy, moderate reform party ready to accept the blessings of the media which still wanted to oppose Drapeau and company. The MCM ran a good campaign, but finished a solid third in media opinion. It came as no surprise that in all districts the MCM's electoral scorecard corresponded to the degree of local involvement and community action it had undertaken in the past. In those neighbourhoods where the MCM had been active in community politics between 1974 and 1978 it did relatively well. In those districts where it was known only through the media, it was crushed.

City-wide, the MCM elected only one councillor, although it received 18 per cent of the vote. The upstart Municipal Action Group passed it by, with 26 per cent, also electing one. The combined opposition vote — 44 per cent — was about what the MCM had achieved in 1974, and a district-by-district breakdown shows that a unified opposition would have taken thirteen seats in 1978.

Of course, we cannot entirely attribute the MCM's downfall during the 1978 elections to the media. The political climate, the split opposition and the work done by the Drapeau organization were definitely the overriding factors. However, there is a moral to this story: Any movement concerned with social transformation through a radical, democratic process has to expect conflict with the dominant social institutions, and consequently needs a clear communication strategy which minimizes its dependence on mainstream media and makes room for the direct participation of ordinary people. On one hand, communication must be something more than propaganda; but on the other, a social movement needs to be immunized against institutionalized distortion, which can too easily come with exclusive and systematic reliance on mass media to get its messages across.

A tentative postscript: The MCM bounced back in 1982 to become the official opposition party at Montreal City Hall, winning fifteen seats and 36 per cent of the vote (compared to thirty-nine seats and 47 per cent for the ruling Civic Party, and three seats and 17 per cent for the third party, MAG). The MCM comeback was in no small measure aided by the strong performance of its mayoralty candidate, CSN labour lawyer Jean Doré. The media labelled Doré as an unknown quantity at the start of the campaign, but he proved to be an excellent communicator, skilled at compressing complex MCM platform points into the concise messages the media can handle. At the same time he did not strip away the political content of those messages. Interestingly, his background includes time spent in the newsroom at Radio-Canada, a stretch as press secretary to René Lévesque, and several seasons as host of a weekly TV program for consumers on Radio-Québec. But the question remained: How far would the MCM be able to go in the future without autonomous means of communication?

5. Spoiling the party: the case of Le Jour

The difficulties and contradictions inherent in establishing alternative communications in contemporary Quebec were readily apparent in the short life of the first daily newspaper to support Quebec independence: *Le Jour*.

Le Jour was born out of the October 1973 provincial elections when the Liberal Party swept the PQ. Headed up by the two main party figures, René Lévesque and Jacques Parizeau, as well as by Yves Michaud, former journalist and ex-MNA, *Le Jour* was designed to give the independence movement a much wider platform than that provided by the National Assembly — where the PQ had only six deputies despite its 30 per cent of the vote.

The opening issue of February 28, 1974 declared that *Le Jour* would also back social-democratic ideals: "This newspaper will be *indépendantiste,* social-democratic, national and free", the editorial announced. The role of *Le Jour* would be to fill the gaps in the availability of information for independence-minded citizens of Quebec.

In addition to these praiseworthy objectives, *Le Jour* also intended to bring in a different administrative model, something similar to *Québec-Presse* (which *Le Jour* had eclipsed). The paper belonged to a company whose five hundred shares would be held by its printer, its typesetter, its journalists, the Parti québécois and different regional committees of the nationalist Société nationale des Québécois.

Le Jour's journalists were also grouped together as an editorial corporation, along the lines of the Paris daily *Le Monde.* The board of directors was composed of nine members, three of whom were journalists. Finally, an editorial board made up of the editor-in-chief, his assistant and two journalists elected by their colleagues made daily editorial decisions. This was the situation in theory. In fact the *Le Jour* journalists experienced less in the way of self-management than their counterparts at *Québec-Presse,* according to Louis Fournier who was involved in both undertakings. [37]

During its thirty-month existence, *Le Jour* was known for its strong pro-independence editorial policy and its spunky reporting. Fierce competition set in between *Le Jour* and *Le Devoir,* reminiscent of the rivalry between *Le Nouveau Journal* and *La Presse* at the beginning of the 1960s. Both papers went after readers who wanted "involved" reporting, and for a time, both papers gave it to them. *Le Jour* conducted a sort of guerrilla war in its editorials against *Le Devoir*'s editor Claude Ryan, a notorious federalist soon to be leader of the Quebec Liberal Party. But when the dust settled, *Le Jour* was unable to supply consistently the kind of in-depth reporting that *Le Devoir* readers had grown accustomed to. News-hungry supporters of independence bought *Le Jour*, but found they could not get along without *Le Devoir* too.

Le Jour's circulation reached thirty thousand copies. *Le Devoir*'s fell to about the same level, but it had an extra advantage: Its federalist sympathies assured it of government advertising, something systematically refused to *Le Jour* despite the protests that erupted when this became known. The Quebec Press Council, in a judgement made public in September 1976, concluded that several ministers were involved in depriving *Le Jour* of its share of government advertising.[38] Strange but true: Though the two papers had the same print-run, *Le Devoir*'s advertising revenues were three times higher than *Le Jour*'s.[39] *Le Jour* thus suffered from the same enforced starvation diet that had killed papers like *Vrai* (Jacques Hébert's anti-Duplessis paper of 1955), *Le Nouveau Journal* and *Québec-Presse*.

All the same, financial problems alone did not kill *Le Jour*.[40] Its death was the result of a hard-fought struggle between journalists and management. Though the project had been launched in an euphoric spirit of service to a common cause — the independence of Quebec — *Le Jour* soon became a battleground for two tendencies within this political option. It was the perfect setting for an inevitable confrontation, similar to so many others that have shaken the independence movement over the years. In effect, the management of *Le Jour* envisioned a traditional capitalist newspaper enterprise (and later, when they found themselves running the State, these same gentlemen would apply the same hierarchical model to the public trust). On the other hand, a majority of the journalists, for whom independence meant more than constitutional modification, wanted the paper to function according to self-management principles. This basic difference spilled over into policy questions, and there were times when the newsroom wanted to take a more critical stance towards the Parti québécois, something that the directors could not stand.[41]

The situation at *Le Jour* worsened during the summer of 1976, especially after the journalists unionized. (Previously they had not deemed unionization necessary because they already had a collective organization, their editorial corporation, which according to the by-laws of the paper gave them an important role in its management.) With the coming provincial elections, the directors decided that all PQ supporters had to close up ranks. After a series of incidents, including the publication on May 1, 1976 of an expression of support for the Common Front of public-sector workers and certain articles showing the PQ in a less than favourable light, the *Le Jour* directors decided to "take charge" of the news pages, which up until then had been the sole responsibility of the journalists. Following a shareholders' meeting on August 10, the editorial corporation (the journalists) lost some of its power while the positions of publisher and editor-in-chief were strengthened to make them correspond to traditional newspapers.

The journalists' determination not to yield to this diminution of their powers — a determination they announced in the paper itself[42] — was the paper's "death sentence". The directors immediately suspended publication on August 24, and simply closed down the paper four days later, rather than let "a handful of troublemakers" run it.[43]

The experience — which had certain similarities with the "liquidations" being practised by the far left around the same time — led some journalists to wonder if they should not have adopted a standard labour-management approach rather than try for self-management.[44] Would that have saved *Le Jour?* Not likely. Even after August 10, journalists at *Le Jour* enjoyed much more power than their colleagues in other enterprises. But once they had got a taste of self-management they wanted more. They were ready to go for broke rather than give in, especially since giving in in this case meant submission, not to an owner, but to a political party.

However, despite the humiliating loss of its party organ only a few months before the general elections, despite also the opposition of all the mainstream media (except for *Le Devoir*), the Parti québécois took power in November 1976. What does that tell us about the power of the media — or lack of it — in the political process?

6. Inside mainstream media: more than fighting words

Awareness of the media's role in maintaining the social system increased in Quebec through the 1970s. As a result, a variety of attempts were made to correct the shortcomings of the mainstream communication networks. Some of these attempts, as we have seen, were sporadic and ephemeral; others were systematic but no more stable. But there was another dimension to the interaction between social movements and means of communication during this time: This had to do with the internal relations within mainstream mass media, institutions not on the fringe of social activity, but at its very heart. In fact, through the 1970s, more and more information workers began casting a critical eye towards the institutions in which they were employed.

Journalists were among the groups targeted by the repression that followed the wave of radicalization in the late sixties and early seventies. At the beginning of 1970, during a union conflict in the Radio-Canada newsroom, news director Marc Thibault declared, "There's no room on Radio-Canada's airwaves for violent or anarchistic opinions. Radio-Canada isn't going to herald in the revolution."[45] A few months later, three reporters were threatened with dismissal if they did not stop working for the pro-independence review *Point de Mire*. One of them, Robert Mackay, refused to submit and was fired. Later in 1970, two militants in the newsroom journalists' union, Michel Bourdon and Denis Vincent, were fired for having criticized Radio-Canada's news policy during the October Crisis.[46] That Crisis hit journalists hard. Quebec's professional journalists' association, the FPJQ, compiled close to three dozen cases of arrests and house searches of journalists in the days following the declaration of the War Measures Act, not counting cases of police and judicial interference in journalists' professional activities.[47] Some journalists were totally in the opposition camp by this time.

Between 1972 and 1975, union and professional organizations of journalists were strengthened, especially the Fédération nationale des communications (FNC), affiliated with the CSN, and the FPJQ. Both these organizations increased their membership and produced important research on a variety of subjects.[48] In general, these groups analyzed the link they saw between their working conditions and the quality of work they produced. This link became the major focal point of the journalists' critique of their work and the social role of journalism in general.

The documents produced by the main organizations within the trade bear out a number of common themes: the public's right to information; the dangers of corporate concentration in the press; the role of the State in information; the control of the practitioner over his or her work; and freedom of information. These themes provided an antithesis to the official principles of the mainstream media: freedom of the press, neutrality of the press and the objectivity of journalistic reporting.

The journalists' organizations thus found themselves aligned against the conventional ideological wisdom of the media. Seeds of conflict inherent to such opposition flowered during this period, mostly through professional pressure and union disputes. Obviously, all Quebec journalists did not skirmish with their bosses, but there was a distinct current of refusal by many to act as neutral channels of information, according to the usual prescribed fate of professional journalists in our type of society.[49]

As mentioned earlier, the union dispute at *La Presse* in 1971 was part and parcel of the journalists' criticism of the quality of information, of corporate concentration in the press and of the need to control the free flow of information during periods of social agitation. In the years following this conflict, especially after the creation of the FNC in 1972, journalists and communication workers in general continued fighting for a kind of information that would serve the interests of the politically disenfranchised rather than a dominant élite. Professional and union issues were combined, and the trade was characterized by vigorous debate between "syndicalists" and "professionals", as supporters of the main tendencies labelled each other.[50] However, behind all the sound and fury, behind all the major union conflicts of the time, important professional issues were raised and there was a new concern for labour relations within professional associations.

Labour trouble increased in the communications sector from 1975 onward and reached a high point in 1977 and 1978, when more than half of all FNC members were either on strike or locked out at the same time. Over three thousand information workers were involved in various conflicts. Besides wages and job security, their demands centred around professional standards and, in certain cases, the recognition of the union.

In 1975, a two-month long conflict at *Le Devoir* resulted in the creation of an information committee made up mostly of union members; its role was to plan, review and evaluate news coverage. The publisher, however, had the right to veto the committee's decisions. At *Le Soleil* in Quebec City, a ten-month strike in 1977-78 centred around union demands that its members' competence be recognized and that they be given jurisdiction over the finished product. And at *La Presse,* during the same time, a strike was called over a seemingly harmless event: the nomination of a sports director against the wishes of the reporters in that department. But the real reasons for the strike were the deterioration of professional relations and a lowering in the quality of information. In reality, "reporter power" was the real issue behind most of these conflicts, and newspaper owners fought the idea with tooth and nail.[51]

The struggles that took place during 1977 and 1978, not only at *La Presse* and *Le Soleil,* but also at Radio-Mutuel, Radio-Québec, *Montréal-Matin* and *The Montreal Star,* were particularly nasty ones, as a page one editorial in *La Presse* demonstrated. The editorial, published on the paper's first day back, was written by publisher Roger Lemelin, one of Quebec's most powerful public-opinion makers.* The frankness with

* Also the author of *Les Plouffe.*

which Lemelin expressed the point of view of certain Quebec employers is remarkable.

With this stroke of its publisher's pen, *La Presse* stripped away its veil of objectivity, took a stand and warned its readers against a very specific adversary: the union movement. According to Lemelin, the strike was:

> an obvious pretext for the union to pursue other goals that reach far beyond *La Presse*. Our paper is only a launching-pad for the CSN's ideological crusade and thirst for power throughout Quebec.
>
> What is the goal of this crusade? Egalitarianism, the class struggle and the pressing of workers from different key sectors of the economy into an awesome Common Front, against which the government can do nothing, and which will lead Quebec into the kind of social anarchy leftists dream of. We also believe it is a direct assault on the concept of private ownership of newspapers and a struggle against all forms of established authority, all except the authority of unions.[52]

The purpose of Lemelin's editorial, so he said, was to warn the population of the danger at hand. The CSN had strategically chosen the journalists, he said, in order to take advantage of their prestige and at the same time to compromise them. The CSN was seeking to control *La Presse* through the journalists' union. Lemelin made the link with other conflicts in the communications sector at the time: "The poison of union militancy is seeping into the Quebec news industry, and if journalists don't have the courage to reject it, their jobs and the freedom of the press will be finished. And without this freedom there will be chaos."[53] Then came another tirade against the CSN and its "crusade for egalitarianism". Lemelin labelled the union central's actions as terrorism and finished up with a claim that in spite of all this he was not anti-union.

Lemelin's article is particularly significant because it laid bare the basis of social conflict on the front page of a major daily. His adversaries could not afford the luxury of such an outburst; they were too concerned with appearing to be reasonable in the public eye, too afraid of being co-opted by far left-wing dogmatism and, in any case, they could not get their hands on such a powerful medium. Lemelin's aggressive style — ranging toward invective — is also interesting for a paradoxical reason: In spite of himself he demystifies that legendary objectivity so dear to the mainstream media.

The conflicts that paralyzed the media in 1977 and 1978 led certain professional and scholarly experts to worry about the critical state of Quebec newspapers. Many well-known figures expressed their opinions publicly, either demanding inquiries or proposing changes of every shape and form.[54] The feeling that a major crisis was imminent drew public attention to the mass media and paved the way for a critical examination of the media's position in society.

But this was not to be the end. In 1980-81, journalists in the Radio-Canada newsroom went on strike for eight months, and *Le Devoir* followed suit over a nine-week period. In both cases, the interruptions in service were the longest in the history of these media. At Radio-Canada, in addition to professional and economic demands the journalists called for "the public's right to information", taking a stand against management's policy and especially its absolutist style.[55] At *Le Devoir*, the conflict centred around respect for the integrity of journalists' articles, the functioning of the information committee and the nomination of editorial executives.[56] In both cases, the conflicts displayed a new hardening of labour relations within the trade, as well as the socio-political nature of journalists' concerns.

Clearly, we haven't heard the last word from Quebec's journalists.

5

TOWARDS DEMOCRATIC COMMUNICATIONS

In any communication system the people who control the making of messages have power over those who receive them. This power can vary according to the origin, function and use of a particular message, but merely being in a position to transmit messages places the sender in a position of domination *vis-à-vis* the receiver.

Part of this power comes from the fact that the sender controls not only the content of the message, but also the language or style. This is readily apparent in the very use of the word "communication", which is employed more and more as a benign replacement for other more concrete expressions such as "information", "message" or "journalism". For instance, as early as 1960 the American journalist and press critic A.J. Liebling noted a trend towards the establishment of "Schools of Communication" and considered how this reflected a change in language:

> Communication means simply getting any idea across and has no intrinsic relation to truth. It is neutral. It can be a pedlar's tool, or the weapon of a political knave, or the medium of a new religion. "Journalism" has a reference to what happens, day by day, but "communication" can deal, just as well, with what has not happened, what the communicator wants to happen, or what he wants the dupe on the other end to think.[1]

In fact, rather than being neutral, the word itself becomes part of the prevailing ideology of objectivity in the communications media. An important part of the social role of the media is to keep afloat the myth of its own neutrality. Social communication is in fact an ideological activity, relying on a system of ideas and values in which, at a given historical moment, a certain number of people recognize themselves and their aspirations. As ideology, communication serves to motivate political and social action, and in this manner it can act as a moving force or catalyst.

The fact that most of the major communication enterprises are owned by large corporations gives a head start to the capitalist system. The fact that in Canada the State owns the rest of them reinforces its role as a maker and promoter of "neutral ideas". By propagating, protecting and reproducing a ruling-class view of the world, mainstream media do their part in suppressing or marginalizing protest movements in the early stages of their development. There is ample evidence of this in the cases covered in this book but, interestingly, most of those cases also illustrate the fact that the media are not quite as monolithic and air-tight — and therefore powerful — as they might seem. On the contrary, their inherent ambiguities make them important battlegrounds.

Contrary to their ideological claims, media institutions have an undeniable class function; nowhere is this more clear than during moments of crisis. In Quebec the Saint-Jean-Baptiste Day riot in 1968, the October Crisis in 1970 and the various *La Presse* strikes were all instances when the media abandoned their usual practices in order to campaign actively for one particular set of social interests. Even in moments of crisis, however, the logic of their imperatives means that the media can be diverted; this happened during the October Crisis and the 1972 general strike in the public sector, when competition with one another compelled the media to cover events in a certain way — and by so doing to grant those events a legitimacy that escaped the media's own control.

At stake on these ideological battlegrounds is either the maintenance or the destruction of the hegemony of the ruling order. In our era, when everyday perceptions of the world are so influenced by mass media production, it is not far-fetched to say that the institutions of mass communication are in the forefront of any system of domination.

1. Senders and receivers: the social role

Social movements that consider themselves as "opposition" need a unified practical and theoretical approach that emphasizes the specific nature of communication while taking into account both the social issues of the day and the movements' overall goals. Contemporary social movements in Quebec, as elsewhere in the Western world, have rarely confronted this question in a head-on, comprehensive manner. Instead they have tended in the heat of battle (and often unconsciously) to develop *de facto* strategies, only partial answers to the problems of communication. In those cases where communication strategies have been explicitly worked out, they have most often fallen into a variety of traps.

For example, a number of movements have been unduly influenced by the erroneous orthodox Marxist notion that ideology is determined by social conditions. According to this view it should be a simple matter to "open the workers' eyes" and they will rise up in revolt against the bourgeoisie. Seen this way, communication is no more than a mechanical operation, a logistical problem. But real life is not so simple, and analysis of concrete communication experiences is one way of demystifying this false and dangerous notion.

The stakes of communication are nothing less than control over the production of social interpretations of reality, yet opposition movements still attack the problem only partially. For some, it is enough to criticize the mainstream media. Others try to create "alternative" media in the hopes that these will replace the old methods of circulating information at least among a certain target group. Still others fight for access to the media, while some progressive individuals attempt to exercise influence from within.

However, few efforts have worked out an overall approach that would bring together the analysis of the social role of the media, the recognized need to propagate alternative information and the awareness of what can be done in different areas of activity. The interesting thing about the Quebec experience of the sixties and seventies is its wealth of different initiatives. Using the knowledge gained from these various enterprises, it should be possible to start building an overall approach. First, however, a few general conclusions:

- Mass communication media are not outside the mainstream of social activity, as they usually claim to be. They are very clearly part of such activity. On the other hand, in spite of their influence, they do not necessarily have the power to determine events, as is often believed. Their importance lies mainly in defining the parameters of public debate and the context of events.

- It is very difficult for alternative commmunication media to survive in mainstream society without becoming part of the traditional private or public sectors. Economic constraints seem to be prohibitive unless the alternative medium is actually the propaganda tool for a specific political organization. However, the mutations taking place in the media industries — for example, the closing down of big-city dailies, the opening up of new TV channels and the changes heralded in consumer habits — point to potential new possibilities as yet difficult to imagine.

- One aspect that should not be neglected among social issues in the communications field is the special role of communication workers, especially journalists. They represent a bridge between media and social movements and their activities can contribute to the opening of new spaces beneficial to opposition-movement interests and useful for limiting the political influence of captial and the State on media enterprises.

2. The cultural reading of messages

The analysis of specific communication experiences demonstrates how the cultural dimension can weigh in the balance during times of social conflict and in history in general. As a whole, alternative communication in Quebec helped created and make flourish a new collective memory, a feeling of solidarity, new ideologies based on new values — in short, a new culture. Indeed, the general effect of these practices has been more cultural than political, and they should be seen as such. Theoretically, this suggests that the cultural approach to communications can be of great interest as a guide to analysis and a tool for strategy.

As a radical alternative to orthodox Marxism, such an approach takes us beyond the classical notion that the "material base" always determines the "superstructure". It considers cultural products to be symbolic models of collective and individual action, and sees the different communication media as platforms for the invention and sharing of social meaning. Mainstream media tend to reinforce the ideology of the material forces that created and control them. In the same way, new means of communication emerging from the opposition can have totally opposite consequences.

Yet even within the mass media there are certain contradictions to be taken into account. Recent studies in semiology have demonstrated that what is communicated during the transmission of a message depends as much on the recipient's reading code as on the speaker's intentions. With this is mind, it is safe to say that there is never just one reading of a message. A recipient reads a message according to his or her own frame of reference, which can be in opposition — or even hostile — to that of the speaker. So, for example, someone whose frame of reference was formed by activist experiences within the union movement — nurtured on *Québec-Presse,* for example — could very easily read *La Presse* through a filter correcting that paper's distortion of messages about the union movement. On the other hand, someone else whose frame of reference was formed only by reading *La Presse* and similar organs would presumably have different attitudes, and draw different conclusions.

The making of an individual's frame of reference is thus of great importance in the social process. The maintenance of the ideological consensus that allows one social group to remain in power depends on the suppression of any nascent oppositional frame of reference. Communication, as a process of sharing common experience, of participation and association, becomes very important in this scheme of things.

The cultural approach to communication considers activities as seemingly banal as reading the paper or watching television as a series of rituals that affirm and maintain a certain perspective on social reality. Putting aside the content of their messages, the ritual itself reinforces the sense of belonging to a culture. This makes communication a symbolic process by which social reality is produced, maintained, repaired and transformed. In short, our consumption of mainstream mass media implicitly supports the ruling system.

In the absence of a critical spirit nourished by interpretations other than those provided by mainstream media, an innocent audience runs the risk of taking this mediated vision of the world as "the truth". The access to *counter-interpretations* is thus an indispensible element of any attempt to question the social status quo. The common thread of the experiences reviewed in this book is that they all involve attempts to create counter-information.

3. Models and strategies for change

If I have not chosen to theorize in these pages about a proper communication strategy for a moment of political rupture, it is because the Quebec experience is too sparse in this regard to provide anything like a blueprint. Also, when it is cut off from a specific context this kind of theorizing becomes useless, and theory should not be invented in the absence of practice.

Some important work, however, has been done in this area by the European sociologist Armand Mattelart, who was involved in Chile during the period of socialist transformation between 1970 and 1973.[2] Mattelart criticizes Salvador Allende's Popular Unity coalition for minimizing the importance of communications in the economic and social transformations it undertook. He points out that a revolutionary change must go beyond "inverting the signs of the message" to explode the sender-receiver relationship. It must reach down into the most submerged levels of society to democratize the communication system and destroy what is fundamentally a relationship of domination. Mattelart conceives of participation in communication as the highest form of popular democracy in a new society. Communication would cease to be the private preserve of professional experts and would begin to be produced by the subjects of history themselves. From then on, ideology would be anchored in lived experience, instead of dominating it.

This framework indicates that scrupulous attention has to be paid to the democratic functioning of media. It leads to a fundamental question: What should be the link between political movements and truly democratic communication? Failure to deal with this question inevitably leads to disappointing results.

The historical review of the Quebec experience done in this book shows how traditional mass media function in our type of society, how different types of alternative practices are limited in their effect, and how anyone who hopes to challenge authority must work out a coherent communication strategy. It does not provide any perfect model for such a strategy, something that would conform to the objectives of social movements. But it is possible to point to certain constants that appear crucial. It is possible to discern the contours of a typical opposition social movement in interaction with communications.

- The typical opposition social movement is born with no particular concern for communication strategies, but new forms of social action inevitably bring with them innovations in communication.

- As they evolve, social movements become critically aware of dominant communication institutions and practices as reflected in the mass media. The evolution of this critical awareness takes place not only in the action of the movements, but also in the social relations inside the media themselves.

- Depending on their position of relative strength, social movements may take concrete steps to influence the situation by developing a coherent communications strategy and practice, consistent with their goals and ideas. They may choose to launch independent means of communication, or even try to establish direct communication with society as a whole.

In this study we have seen two main types of movements. One made communication the mainspring of its overall strategy (the union movement, the far left-wing political groups). The other tried to work towards social change without a conscious communication strategy (most popular and community groups, attempts at political consolidation such as FRAP and the Montreal Citizens' Movement). Groups in the first category often ended up politically subordinating communication to propaganda purposes, while those of the second type often reduced communication to the mere seeking of mass media favour.

Between these two extremes, at least three other types of communication practices characterized the various social movements in Quebec: alternative media (*Parti pris, Québec-Presse,* the Agence de presse libre du Québec); direct action (during the October Crisis of 1970 and the public sector strikes of 1972); and action aimed at the mainstream media (demystifying the media through critical "exposés", reform struggles of journalists' unions and professional groups).

The concept of "alternative communication practices", as a cultural phenomenon, can also be used as a way of distinguishing between these different types of experiences. This concept goes against the idea of communication as political propaganda (that is, as promotion for a specific political organization). Attempts at propaganda have sought to use strategies and machinations reminiscent of sloppy television commercials. Propaganda is the antithesis of democratic, two-way communication; it cannot substitute for a popular culture. In the Quebec experience it appeared for a time that the Agence de presse libre du Québec might get close to launching a communication network in which the communicators would have been interchangeable — but then the APLQ was diverted from its attempt.

To illustrate this, it is useful to take another look at the magazine *Mobilisation*'s summing up of ten years of Quebec propaganda efforts. *Mobilisation* considered the *Parti pris*/MLP experiences of the mid-1960s as a failed attempt to link ideological practice and the building of a party. (It should be pointed out, however, that *Parti pris* succeeded as a cultural catalyst where it failed as a political organization.) In the FLP, *Mobilisation* saw a directionless mass propaganda effort. It saw in the FLQ and FRAP two failures to clearly redefine political orientations, and in the case of the APLQ, an example of ideological weakness. *Mobilisation* even set itself apart from the *Bulletin populaire* — the project with which it had the most in common. *Mobilisation*'s differences with all these groups was based on the fact that it was the first to totally subordinate ideological activity to political goals. In so doing it imitated one of the basic aspects of the bourgeois press, a feature it had found so outrageous: It pretended to be dealing in objective truth. *Mobilisation*, with all its rigour, led directly to the "liquidation" of a number of important ideological instruments of the left in the mid-1970s (including itself).

This is obviously not an acceptable approach, for both political and practical reasons. The creation of a vanguard party is not what will lead to the threshold of liberation. Once again, such a notion only repeats the relations of domination it purports to denounce in the present system, relations based on centralizing and centralized power. It was the number one trap on the left in Quebec in 1970s, and many communication projects fell into it.

On the contrary, what is most needed is the formation of a coherent link between the goals of social movements and their communication strategies. A medium designed to serve a political movement that is socialist, democratic and anti-authoritarian must:
- create a feeling of belonging to a common culture;
- challenge mainstream media by providing its audience with alternative interpretations of reality;
- practise self-management in its internal workings and be controlled by a general assembly of owner-members;
- be independent of both business interests and the State;
- have links with popular, political and union movements without being organically tied to them.

Though only in a partial way, *Québec-Presse* probably came closest to this model. It is certainly not by accident that seven years after the demise of *Québec-Presse*, the Communications

Work Group of the ICEA — one of the rare research and study groups in Quebec dealing with these questions on a regular basis — chose the earlier project as a way of rekindling the debate about communication alternatives.

The history of *Québec-Presse* published by the ICEA on May Day 1981 shows just how symbiotic a relationship the paper had with the Quebec left of the late 1960s. Did the left create *Québec-Presse*, or did the paper create the left as "a widely based coalition of forces of change"? Despite the enormous financial and political difficulties that culminated in the paper's collapse, no one can deny the importance of this project in building a new culture — one that continues to exist today.

Indeed, the cultural sphere has a certain autonomy from political victories and defeats. In the cultural sphere, lasting effects are to be found in people's consciousness. In communications, once the basic information is transmitted — once everyone knows where the demonstration is going to take place or whom they should vote for (or why they shouldn't vote) — something less tangible, but more important, remains. A pair of press clippings from 1980 provides a few hints as to what this is. First, from an article in *Le Devoir* reporting on "an evening in honour of Paul Rose":

> The under-thirties were rather rare on stage, although they were in the majority in the audience. The young people had come to find out about events they had never experienced quite consciously. The high point of the evening came when the giant video screen flashed with the famous reading by Gaétan Montreuil of the FLQ Manifesto, first broadcast on Radio-Canada on October 8, 1970.
>
> The artists present each commented in their own way on the events of ten years ago. Almost all spoke first-hand of arrest and detention, declaring that the resistance of the *Québécois* people is far from stifled. With the hindsight of the years, one realizes how important these events have been on the political maturation of the *Québécois:* at least, that is what some observers think.[3]

Second, a report quoting the words of *Québécois* singer Paul Piché:

> Sure I sing about misery and poverty and industrial diseases, and I'm in perfect health, I'm living well, I'm not out on the street. That doesn't matter. What's important is the encouragement I can offer people. One of the best compliments I ever got came from a guy in Thetford Mines who couldn't believe it when he heard a song about industrial diseases on the radio. Of course it's true I'm trying to increase my own popularity, but I do it by circulating progressive ideas and if I can get enough people behind those causes, it could get dangerous and things might start to change.[4]

Perhaps more tangible are the independent media that provide another form of political involvement in the cultural arena. In the early 1980s there was a brief but certain renaissance of the left-wing press in Quebec, with the appearance of projects more restrained and less ambitious than *Québec-Presse* or the APLQ, but subscribing to similar principles. Neighbourhood newspapers such as *Liaison-St-Louis* in Montreal, some community radio stations, magazines like the monthly *Le Temps Fou* (1978-1983), the feminist *La Vie en Rose*, the newsjournal *presse libre* (1981-82), and numerous even smaller, specialized publications, tried to carry on the tradition.

Far from being similar, either in form or content, these projects shared one important common characteristic. They were all situated politically between the two major options of bolshevism and social democracy, which paralyzed the Quebec left in the late 1970s and reached a peak during the first mandate of the Parti québécois.

The arrival of the PQ in power in 1976 and the rise of the authoritarian left around the same time had an anaesthetizing effect on many social movements. Disillusionment with both by the early 1980s offered hope of renewal, and the more recent communication projects were signs of new forms of mobilization to come.*

---

* As this book goes to press two new reviews have just appeared on Quebec newsstands: *Mouvements,* published by the Quebec Teachers' Union (CEQ); and *Idées et pratiques alternatives,* produced by an editorial collective. A number of other projects are known to be on the drawing boards.

This look at the role of the mainstream media and alternative communication in Quebec makes it easier to appreciate the link between political action and cultural communication. This link implies, in my view, that anyone interested in political intervention has to pay close attention to formulating a clear communication strategy, coherent with political objectives. The history of the 1970s is littered with failed attempts to create political alternatives while continuing to use communication as propaganda or restricting it to a conventional use of mass media. A good example is the PQ itself, which "succeeded" in establishing a legitimate foothold in the media, but only once it had sufficiently transformed itself to fit easily into the media's prescribed mould.

Now that the left is more aware of the stakes involved in communications, it should be concerned to find new forms of action, or at least to modify the already familiar forms. Both in mainstream and independent media, alternative practices can help progressive causes. Mass media institutions, as we've seen, are ideological battlegrounds in which different types of practice compete with each other to define the limits of public debate. We have also seen how small independent media act as cultural vehicles circulating critical interpretations of reality. Can new technologies contribute to breaking down the traditional sender-receiver model and help transform the social relations of communication?

One thing is certain: The question of communication demands a critical, multi-faceted and dialectical approach that takes all these elements into account. When it comes to communication practice, choices have to be made which take into account available resources and theatres of action. In general the job is to find the proper forum for each particular circumstance, without excluding any possibility out of hand. The task of synthesizing political action and cultural communication may be the leading challenge facing social movements today. The strategies they use to accept that challenge will have much to say about the creative imagination of social movements — and their ability to act.

APPENDIX I:
CONSCIOUS OMISSIONS

The emphasis in this study has been on large-scale communications projects, generalized phenomena and the major turning points in Quebec's social history of the 1960s and 1970s. There are, however, a number of areas of experience I did not venture into but which, each in its own way, illustrates the richness of alternative communication practices and would no doubt make interesting subjects of study on their own.

The regions

It might be said that this study suffers from a "metropolitan" prejudice in favour of Montreal. Indeed, I recognize that the importance of the "little media" increases as one travels further from the centre. The period under consideration is ripe with attempts to build independent media in all areas of Quebec. Some of the more important ones have been studied elsewhere.

In Saint-Jérôme, for instance, there were several important experiences: the paper *Résistance,* community-oriented cinema, and participation of activists in community television. All this was documented in Michel Beauchamp's *Initiatives militantes et communication,* Quebec City, CEQ, 1974.

A local group in Abitibi attempted to create a popular communication network known as *Le Bloc* as a means of politicizing and promoting a regional culture. This was described in Beauchamp, *op. cit.,* and in Barbier-Bouvet *et al., op. cit.*

In Eastern Quebec, in addition to the BAEQ's well-known projects, activists took a variety of other initiatives, especially under the auspices of "Operation Dignity". See Benoît Lévesque, *Les communications et le développement, loc. cit.*, and Gilles Godin and Jacques Langlois, "La voix du peuple," in Lévesque (ed.), *op. cit.*, pp. 115-121.

The counter-culture

Cultural questions, already on the agenda for the left in the 1960s, were especially notable in the writings of certain members of the *Parti pris* group. See, for example, Pierre Maheu, "Vers une culture québécoise responsable," *Socialisme 67* (12-13) April-May-June 1967, pp. 55-58; and the important article by Luc Racine, Narcisso Pizarro, Michel Pichette and Gilles Bourque, "Production culturelle et classes sociales au Québec", *Parti pris* 4, (9-12) May-June-July-August 1967, pp. 43-75.

But it was not until the 1970s that these issues emerged from the marginality of radical circles with the attempts to bring culture out of the fine arts academies, to launch collective, self-managing creative projects and to protest the bureaucratic approach to culture. For several examples, see Côté and Harnois, *op. cit.*

I have not paid much attention here to what is called the counter-culture, the culture of young protesters. This was the first opposition movement in Quebec to go beyond class analysis as the basis of its activities. As a movement of ideas and a meeting-place of communication and other social practices, the counter-culture was a promoter of social change clearly in opposition to dominant ideologies. See Serge Proulx's article, *loc. cit.*, referred to in the introduction. In the most active period, from 1967-72, dozens of counter-culture publications appeared and disappeared like falling stars. The most important of these were *Le Quartier Latin* and *Mainmise*.

Le Quartier Latin grew out of the University of Montreal student paper of the same name and attempted from 1969 to 1971 to establish a link between the active radical youth and popular and union movements. The orthodox left — in fact nothing more than the preceding generation of young militants — criticized *Le Quartier Latin* for its spontaneity and lack of ideological precision. Yet the old left also had to acknowledge the paper's outstanding success: 30,000 copies printed every two weeks until the fire went out after the October 1970 wave of repression. In an interview with *Québec-Presse*, Roméo Bouchard, the paper's publisher, placed the review in the context of the social upheaval of Quebec in 1970:

> We figure there are 20,000 young people in Quebec who've left school, who've left their families too for the most part. They're on the road, working a little, stealing for a living. They want to live outside the structures of school, the family, the workplace. They want to live new values and they're not asking anyone's permission. They form communication networks amongst themselves, nobody knows exactly how, but it happens, and put all these networks together and you've got a parallel movement, a sort of libertarian movement, a real danger for industrialized society that functions according to the necessarily repressive rules of efficiency. (Quoted in Maurice L. Roy, "*Le Quartier Latin:* Un journal contesté mais que les jeunes achètent," *Québec-Presse,* May 22, 1970).

After the paper dissolved in 1971, some of its participants became involved in the Agence de presse libre du Québec. Genealogists will note that after the split in the APLQ in 1973, the former *Quartier Latin* members were the ones to leave, later to turn up on the editorial committee that created *Le Temps Fou* in 1978. Serge Martel, for one, was first in charge of distribution for *Le Quartier Latin*, then helped launch the APLQ, and later became one of the founders of *Le Temps Fou,* where he was in charge of administration until 1981.

On the other hand, the journal *Mainmise* was less political from the start. Yet between 1970 and 1978 it was the major representative of the counter-culture in Quebec and enjoyed great popular success. As a monthly, after October 1971, it had a regular distribution of some 26,000 copies. *Mainmise*'s concept of society was libertarian, based on individualism and demanding popular control without any particular political organization. It was always careful to keep a distance from the protest movements that spent those years building the new left-wing orthodoxy whose ups and downs have been charted in this book. See Marie-France Moore, "*Mainmise,* version québécoise de la contre-culture," *Recherches sociographiques* 14 (3), 1973, pp. 363-381.

Despite their apolitical appearance, the communication projects of the counter-culture helped denounce and demystify society's sacred cows, and contributed to building a counter-ideology and political consciousness well beyond a narrow aseptic class consciousness. Most of all, they helped formulate alternatives to both the traditional "power" and the "counter-power" proposed by the orthodox left. The counter-culture instead operated a free zone of "anti-power" (Proulx's idea, *loc. cit.*).

The women's movement

This study has not included the spawning and growth of the women's movement in Quebec, which took root during the 1970s and has doubtlessly had a lasting influence upon society at large.

Besides the specific forms of action and original analyses that it developed, the women's movement also created its own dynamics of communication. A flood of bulletins and publications issued from the movement in the 1970s: *Québécoises debouttes, Pluri-elles, Des luttes et des rires des femmes, Têtes de pioche.* The women's movement also helped establish bookstores, publishing houses, meeting places, information centres and groups of all sorts, including independent "caucuses" within community, political and union groups. The independent magazine *La Vie en Rose,* born in 1981, is typical of this current. Its explicit goal is to recover space denied to feminist culture by the mainstream media, in spite of the occasional welcome mat the media may set out when women become "outraged" enough. See Sylvie Dupont, "La place des femmes dans l'information," in ICEA, *op. cit.*, pp. 12-16.

The English-speaking minority

Finally, I have also not covered the communication experiences of the non-French-speaking minorities in Quebec, the most important of which are the Anglophones.

On the one hand, the mainstream English media played a traditional role of opinion leader to their clientele, which as a whole has held a conservative position in Quebec society. Yet during the period under consideration in this book, pockets of resistance appeared within the English community — and they often sprung up around particular publications, such as the student paper *McGill Daily,* the newsmagazine *Last Post* and the political review *Our Generation* (the oldest left-wing review in Quebec, it has published without interruption since 1961).

These projects, among others, helped an entire generation of non-Francophone *Québécois* to get involved with the social struggles of "the majority".

APPENDIX 2: CHRONOLOGY OF EVENTS

	Society	Mainstream Media	Alternative Media
1958		Journalists' strike at *La Presse*	
1959	Death of Duplessis	Producers' strike at Radio-Canada	*Revue socialiste* launched
1960	Lesage elected: Quiet Revolution begins		
	CSN created		
1961		G. Pelletier named editor-in-chief at *La Presse*	
		Nouveau Journal launched	
1962	Liberals' majority in the polls increased	*Nouveau Journal* fails	
1963	First signs of disillusionment with the Quiet Revolution:		*Parti pris* launched
	Beginning of "social animation"		
	First FLQ activities		

	Society	Mainstream Media	Alternative Media
1964	Ministry of Education created	Union conflict at *La Presse*	*Révolution québécoise* launched
			Socialisme launched
	Labour Code reformed; massive unionization of the public sector	*Journal de Montréal* launched	*La p. . . libre* published by *La Presse* journalists
1965	First citizens' committees appear	G. Pelletier fired from *La Presse*	*Révolution québécoise* integrated into *Parti pris*
	MLP created		
1966	record number of strikes in Quebec	P. Desmarais buys *La Presse*	
	re-emergence of the FLQ		
	Union nationale takes power		
1967	TEVEC launched		first popular newspaper is published: *L'Opinion Ouvrière* of Saint-Henri
	René Lévesque leaves the Liberals		
1968	PQ created		*Parti pris* dissolves

	Society	Mainstream Media	Alternative Media
	Saint Jean-Baptiste Day riot, Montreal	Information policy of *La Presse*, Radio-Canada, etc. questioned by information workers	
	Trudeau elected		Radio-Québec is launched
	CSN's "Second Front" launched		
	first popular information/communication groups launched		
1969	FLP created	Parliamentary Commission on Freedom of the Press in Quebec	*Mobilisation* launched
	first CAPs created	FPJQ created	*Point de Mire* launched
	State applies legal and police pressure against popular opposition	Senate committee investigates Canadian mass media	*Québec-Presse* launched
1970	Bourassa leads the Liberals back to power	Employers and police apply pressure against professional journalists	The FLQ works directly on the communications system
	FRAP created		
	October Crisis: Opposition repressed		

	Society	Mainstream Media	Alternative Media
1971	State begins co-opting movements: OFY and LIP (federal), social service reform (provincial)		APLQ launched
	Radicalization of popular and union movements		
	Common front created by unions	Union trouble at *La Presse*	*Quotidien populaire* published by *La Presse* journalists
1972	Public-sector common front and general strike	FNC created	*Mobilisation* begins publishing "second series"
	creation of community groups involved in ideological work		*Point de Mire* disappears
	implantation of Marxist-Leninist political groups		
1973	CSN splits; CSD created		*Bulletin populaire* launched
	Liberals sweep provincial elections		*Mobilisation* begins publishing "third series"
			Le Jour is launched

	Society	Mainstream Media	Alternative Media
1974	new movements appear; MCM is launched and participates in municipal election		*Québec-Presse* dissolves
1975	union solidarity continues to break down		growth of community media financed by the State
	the State's social reforms are solidified		growth of small community media and independent unions
	Marxist-Leninists increase their influence		
1976	"liquidation" of popular groups, especially ideologically based ones		*Bulletin populaire* and *Mobilisation* liquidated
	PQ takes power	*Le Jour* dissolved	
1977	political polarization between PQ sympathizers and M-L groups paralyzes the popular movement	a spate of union conflicts in several media: *La Presse, Le Soleil*, Radiomutuel, Radio-Québec...	
	a "third way" is sought by the new protest movement		attempts at establishing small independent media

	Society	Mainstream Media	Alternative Media
1978	MCM defeated at the polls	Montréal-Matin closed	Le Temps Fou launched
1979	the referendum takes up most political energies	The Montreal Star closed	a people's colloquium held on the role of the media ("La parole, ça se prend")
1980	Referendum and Constitutional Debate	Union conflict at Radio-Canada	
1981	PQ re-elected	Union conflict at Le Devoir	La Vie en Rose launched Presse libre launched Publication of a "commemorative issue" of Québec-Presse

NOTES*

Chapter 1   Media and Social Change in Quebec: An Overview

[1] Jean-Louis Roy, *La marche des Québécois: Le temps des ruptures, 1945-1960* (Ottawa: Leméac, 1976).

[2] *Ibid.*, pp. 376-378.

[3] Serge Proulx, "Québec 1945-1980: générations politiques, contre-culture, nouveaux mouvements", in Serge Proulx and Pierre Vallières, eds., *Changer de société* (Montreal: Québec-Amérique, 1982).

[4] Roch Denis, *Luttes des classes et question nationale au Québec, 1948-1968* (Montreal: Presses socialistes internationales, 1979).

[5] See Michel Roy, "La grève des réalisateurs de Radio-Canada", *Relations industrielles* 14 (2), April 1959, pp. 265-276; and Pierre Godin, *L'information-opium: Une histoire politique du journal "La Presse"* (Montreal: Parti pris, 1972).

[6] Denis, *op. cit.*

[7] Denis Monière, *Le développement des idéologies au Québec des origines à nos jours* (Montreal: Québec-Amérique, 1977).

[8] Dorval Brunelle, *La désillusion tranquille* (Montreal: Hurtubise HMH, 1978).

[9] Proulx, *loc. cit.*

[10] Norman Penner, *The Canadian Left: A Critical Analysis* (Scarborough: Prentice-Hall, 1977).

[11] Monière, *op. cit.*

[12] Denis, *op. cit.*, p. 360.

[13] Hélène David, "L'état des rapports de classe au Québec de 1945 à 1967", *Sociologie et sociétés* 7 (2), November 1975, pp. 33-66.

[14] This is Brunelle's interpretation, *op. cit.*

[15] David, *loc. cit.*, p. 54.

* Unless otherwise indicated, all French sources have been translated by the translator.

[16] Brunelle, *op. cit.*, p. 198.

[17] See Frédéric Lesemann and Michel Thiénot, *Les animations sociales au Québec* (Montreal: Université de Montréal, École de service social, 1972); Charles Côté and Yannik G. Harnois, *L'animation sociale au Québec: Sources, apports et limites* (Montreal: Éditions coopératives Albert Saint-Martin, 1978); Donald McGraw, *Le développement des groupes populaires à Montréal, 1963-1973* (Montreal: Éditions coopératives Albert Saint-Martin, 1978).

[18] Côté and Harnois, *op. cit.*, p. 141.

[19] *Ibid.*, p. 209.

[20] Lesemann and Thiénot, *op. cit.*

[21] See Gérald Fortin, "Notes de recherche: Les changements d'attitude et de personnalité produits par l'animation sociale et les mass média", *Recherches sociographiques* 9 (3), September-December 1968, pp. 310-312; see also Benoît Lévesque, "Les communications et le développement", *Possibles* 2 (2/3), Winter-Spring 1978, pp. 79-96.

[22] McGraw, *op. cit.*

[23] For a theoretical summing-up of communication experiences among popular groups, see Benoît Lévesque, "Sens politique de l'animation sociale et des communications dans les organismes communautaires et coopératives", in Benoît Lévesque, ed., *Animation sociale, entreprises communautaires et coopératives* (Montreal: Éditions coopératives Albert Saint-Martin, 1979), pp. 318-334.

[24] B.R., journalist, "Une information 'totalitaire' prise à son propre piège", in Jean-Marc Piotte, ed., *Québec-occupé* (Montreal: Parti pris, 1971), pp. 179-216; and "L'information au Québec: de la politique à la consommation", *Socialisme québécois* (21-22), April 1971, pp. 79-108.

[25] McGraw, *op. cit.*, p. 161.

[26] See, for example, Charles Gagnon, "Nécessité de la lutte sur le front idéologique", in *Pour le parti prolétarien* (Montreal: L'Équipe du journal, 1972), pp. 27-44.

[27] Proulx, *loc. cit.*, p. 7.

[28] Marielle Désy, Marc Ferland, Benoît Lévesque and Yves Vaillancourt, *La conjoncture au Québec au début des années 80: les enjeux pour le mouvement ouvrier et populaire* (Rimouski: Librairie socialiste de l'est du Québec, 1980).

[29] Their evaluation is shared by Monière, *op. cit.*; see also Pierre Hamel and Jean-François Léonard, *Les organisations populaires, l'État et la démocratie* (Montreal: Nouvelle optique, 1981).

[30] See McGraw, *op. cit.*; Jacques Godbout and Jean-Pierre Collin, *Les organismes populaires en milieu urbain: contre-pouvoir ou nouvelle pratique professionnelle?* (Montreal: INRS-Urbanisation, 1977).

[31] Côté and Harnois, *op. cit.*

32 Proulx, *loc. cit.*

33 Gérard Pelletier, "The strike and the press", in Pierre Elliott Trudeau, ed., *The Asbestos Strike* (Toronto: James Lorimer and Company, 1974).

34 Gilbert Maistre, "Aperçu socio-économique de la presse quotidienne québécoise", *Recherches sociographiques* 12 (1), January-April 1971, pp. 105-115 (p. 107).

35 *Ibid.*

36 Jacques Benjamin, "Pouvoir politique et médias au Québec", *Communication et Information* 3 (1), 1979, pp. 67-77.

37 "L'information, une arme idéologique", *Parti pris* 2 (2), October 1964, pp. 2-4 (p. 3).

38 On this subject see "Les véritables maîtres de Québec", *Maintenant* (86), May 1969, pp. 144-155.

39 Special Senate Committee on Mass Media, *Mass Media* (Ottawa: Queen's Printer, 1970).

40 *Royal Commission on Newspapers* (Ottawa: Ministry of Supply and Services Canada, 1981), p. 29.

41 Michel Dubé, "Les propriétaires des médias (2): La propriété des médias électroniques au Québec et au Canada", in ICEA, *La parole ça se prend* (Montreal: CEQ/ICEA, 1980), pp. 88-99.

42 Michel Nadeau, "Civitas s'attaque au marché anglophone pour préparer une expansion nord-américaine", *Le Devoir,* November 12, 1980.

43 Gérald Godin, "Les amis de *Québec-Presse* et la censure", *Québec-Presse,* October 22, 1972.

44 Pierre Fournier, "Institutional Penetration: The Case of the Media", chapter 6 of *The Quebec Establishment* (Montreal: Black Rose Books, 1976), pp. 98-108.

45 Wallace Clement, "The Media Elite: Gatekeepers of Ideas", and "Structure and Concentration of Canada's Mass Media", chapters 7 and 8 in *The Canadian Corporate Elite: An Analysis of Economic Power* (Toronto: McClelland and Stewart, 1975), pp. 270-286 and 287-324.

46 Special Senate Committee, *op. cit.*

47 Barry Gruman, "Good reading for shareholders", *Financial Post* supplement, November 19, 1977.

48 CSN, *Boycottons Radiomutuel* (Montreal: CSN, 1977).

49 Multi-Réso, Inc., *La presse écrite au Québec: Bilan et prospective* (Quebec City: Ministère des Communications, 1977).

50 "Profits records pour le canal 10", *Le Devoir,* July 13, 1978.

51 Michel Nadeau, "Les journaux québécois de Péladeau ont réalisé $12 millions de profits", *Le Devoir,* January 22, 1981.

52 *Royal Commission,* pp. 84, 164.

[53] Study carried out by Martin Goldfarb Consultants for the Special Senate Committee, quoted in *op. cit.*, volume III.

[54] *The Public's View*, a study carried out by Communications Research Centre, quoted in *Royal Commission*, pp. 34-36.

[55] Société de recherche en sciences de comportement (SORECOM) Inc., *Enquête sur la diffusion de l'information au Québec* (Quebec City: Commission parlementaire spéciale sur les problèmes de la liberté de la presse, Assemblée nationale du Québec, 1972), p. 12.

[56] *Op. cit.*

[57] Clement, *op. cit.*, p. 198.

[58] *Royal Commission*, p. 182.

[59] Multi-Réso, *op. cit.*

[60] Sylvie Desjardins, "Les propriétaires des médias (1): Portrait de la concentration dans la presse écrite au Canada", in ICEA, *op. cit.*, pp. 71-87; and Nadeau, *loc. cit.*, 2.

[61] *Royal Commission*, p. 101.

[62] B.R., journalist, *loc. cit.*, (2), pp. 104-106.

[63] FPJQ, *Mémoire sur la liberté de presse au Québec* (Montreal: FPJQ, 1972).

[64] Fournier, *op. cit.*

[65] ICEA, *op. cit.* See also the ICEA paper presented to the Royal Commission on Newspapers (Kent Commission), "La concentration et le contrôle de l'information", Montreal, 1980.

Chapter 2   Towards a Parallel Press Movement

[1] P. Godin, *op. cit.*, p. 123.

[2] This short history of *La Presse* from 1958 to 1964 is based on P. Godin, *op. cit.*

[3] P. Godin, *op. cit.*, p. 113.

[4] *Ibid.*, p. 123.

[5] *Ibid.*, p. 140.

[6] Brunelle, *op. cit.*, p. 198.

[7] Jean Hamelin and André Beaulieu, "Aperçu du journalisme québécois d'expression française", *Recherches sociographiques* 7 (3), September-December 1966, pp. 305-348 (p. 340).

[8] See Gilles Mathieu, "Le journalisme et la lutte des classes", *Révolution québécoise* 1 (2), October 1964, pp. 28-34.

[9] David, *loc. cit.*, p. 54.

[10] Brunelle, *op. cit.*, p. 200.

[11] See Jean Rochefort, "La verité sur *La Presse*", *Révolution québécoise* 1 (3), November 1964, pp. 6-11.

[12] *Ibid.*, p. 9.

[13] Pierre Vallières, *La liberté en friche* (Montreal: Québec-Amérique, 1979), p. 17.

[14] See, for example, Penner, *op. cit.*

[15] Roch Denis, *op. cit.*, p. 360.

[16] Robert Major, *Parti pris: Idéologies et littérature* (Montreal: Hurtubise HMH, 1979), p. 5.

[17] Quoted in Vallières, *op. cit.*, p. 17.

[18] Political scientist Anne Legaré has pointed out how important and relevant a group of articles on class analysis can be to a collectivity's political memory in "Heures et promesses d'un débat: les analyses des classes au Québec (1960-1980)", *Les cahiers du socialisme* (5), Spring 1980, pp. 60-84.

[19] See Denis, *op. cit.*

[20] See Charles Gagnon's article, "Classe et conscience de classe", *Socialisme 69* (18), July-August-September 1969, pp. 66-74.

[21] See Luc Racine and Roch Denis, "La conjoncture politique québécoise depuis 1960", *Socialisme québécoise* (21-22), April 1971, pp. 17-78.

[22] Denis, *op. cit.*, p. 546.

[23] *Mobilisation,* first series, (1).

[24] This example is given in a book by Sheilagh Hodgins Milner and Henry Milner, *The Decolonization of Quebec: An Analysis of Left-Wing Nationalism* (Toronto: McClelland and Stewart, 1973).

[25] Jean-Marc Piotte, "Le syndicalisme au Québec depuis 1960", in *Le syndicalisme de combat* (Montreal: Éditions coopératives Albert Saint-Martin, 1977), pp. 85-123.

[26] For this section see Côté and Harnois, *op. cit.;* Lesemann and Thiénot, *op. cit.;* McGraw, *op. cit.;* Désy et al., *op. cit.*

[27] Désy et al., *op. cit.*

[28] CSN, *Le Deuxième Front,* Marcel Pépin's state-of-the-union address to the CSN Convention (Montreal: CSN, 1968).

[29] *Ibid.*, p. 29.

[30] *Ibid.*, p. 47.

[31] Richard Daignault has written an article on the specific problems the union movement had in the field of information at the time: "Les syndicats et l'information du public", in *Le public et l'information en relations de travail* (Quebec City: Les presses de l'Université Laval, Département des relations industrielles, 1969), pp. 96-116.

[32] See the Special Parliamentary Commission on freedom of the press, *Rapport préliminaire: Les travaux de la commission en 1969* (Quebec City: Assemblée nationale du Québec, 1972). A bibliography of the briefs submitted to the Commission can be found in André Versailles, *Communications* (Montreal: Conseil de développement social du Montréal Métropoli-

tain, 1972). See also the dossier in the magazine *Maintenant, loc. cit.*, and "Dossier: Information et enfermement culturel", *Socialisme 69* (17), April-May-June 1969, pp. 58-128.

[33] See Jean Côté, *La communication au Québec* (Repentigny: Point de Mire, 1974).

[34] See François Béliveau, *Pogné* (Montreal: Éditions québécoises, 1971). Also see Marc Raboy, "La tour infernale: la petite histoire de l'information à Radio-Canada", *Le Temps Fou* (14), April-May 1981, pp. 18-22.

[35] See "Dossier: Qui contrôle les moyens d'information?", *Bulletin* (APLQ) (19), July 22-29, 1971.

Chapter 3   Independent Media: The Alternatives

[1] See Normand Caron, "Mais où est donc passé *Québec-Presse*", in *Dossiers "Vie Ouvrière"* 28 (125), May 1978, pp. 288-291.

[2] *Québec-Presse,* March 15, 1970.

[3] *Québec-Presse,* January 25, 1970.

[4] *Québec-Presse,* April 26, 1970.

[5] See Caron, *loc. cit.*

[6] "Le FLQ et nous", *Québec-Presse,* October 11, 1970.

[7] *Québec-Presse,* December 20, 1970.

[8] Caron, *loc. cit.,* p. 288.

[9] G. Godin, *loc. cit.*

[10] See "4 ans", *Québec-Presse,* October 28, 1973; and "*Québec-Presse* fêtera-t-il ses 5 ans?", *Québec-Presse,* October 6, 1974.

[11] See, for example, Roch Denis, "*Québec-Presse* doit se brancher", *Québec-Presse,* October 27, 1974.

[12] See, for example, B.R., journalist, *loc. cit.* (2).

[13] Caron, *loc. cit.,* p. 291.

[14] For a more personal view, see Louis Fournier, "Une expérience de presse engagée: *Québec-Presse,* il y a 10 ans", *Le "30"* 3 (3), March 1979, p. 22.

[15] See *Québec-Presse,* May 1, 1981, published as a special issue of the bulletin of the ICEA, 4 (5), May 1981.

[16] This section is based on Lesemann and Thiénot, *op. cit.;* and on McGraw, *op. cit.*

[17] See Marc Laurendeau, *Les Québécois violents* (Montreal: Boréal Express, 1974).

[18] This is the belief expressed by Daniel Latouche in "Mass Media and Communications in a Canadian Political Crisis", in Benjamin Singer, ed., *Communications in Canadian Society* (Toronto: Copp Clark, 1975), pp. 374-385. Latouche's ideas are re-examined in Arthur Siegel, *Canadian Newspaper Coverage of the FLQ Crisis: A Study of the Impact of the Press on Politics,*

PhD thesis (Montreal: Department of Political Science, McGill University, 1974).

[19] B.R., journalist, *loc. cit.*, (1).

[20] See Siegel, *op. cit.*, and also *Québec-Presse*, December 6, 1970.

[21] Siegel, *op. cit.*

[22] See B.R., journalist, *loc. cit.*, (1).

[23] This section is based on articles published in *Québec-Presse*, October 11, 1970, and in *Last Post*, "October 1970: The Santo Domingo of Pierre Elliott Trudeau", reprinted in Nick auf de Maur and Robert Chodos, eds., *Quebec: A Chronicle, 1968-1972* (Toronto: James Lewis and Samuel, 1972), pp. 49-75.

[24] *Last Post, loc. cit.*

[25] *Québec-Presse, loc. cit.*

[26] *Ibid.*

[27] *Last Post, loc. cit.*

[28] *Ibid.*

[29] *Last Post, loc. cit.*, pp. 61, 63.

[30] "Le FLQ et nous", *Québec-Presse, loc. cit.*

[31] See Latouche, *loc. cit.*

[32] Gérard Pelletier, *La crise d'octobre* (Montreal: Éditions du Jour, 1971).

[33] Siegel, *op. cit.*

[34] *Ibid.*

[35] *Ibid.*, pp. 183-184.

[36] *Québec-Presse*, November 8, 1970.

[37] See, for example, B.R., journalist, *loc. cit.*, (2).

[38] "Editorial: la crise d'octobre 1970 au Québec", *Socialisme québécois* (21-22), April 1971, pp. 5-16 (p. 15).

[39] B.R., journalist, *loc. cit.*, (2), p. 107.

[40] See Désy, *et al., op. cit.*

[41] See Lorne Huston, "Les fleurs du pouvoir", in Lesemann and Thiénot, *op. cit.*, pp. 275-293; and Jean-Robert Sansfaçon and Louise Vandelac, *Perspectives-Jeunesse: Le programme cool d'un gouvernement too much* (Montreal: APLQ, 1972).

[42] See Jean-Guy Lacroix and Benoît Lévesque, "L'unification et la fragmentation des appareils idéologiques au Canada et au Québec: le cas de la radio-télévision", *Les cahiers du socialisme* (5), Spring 1980, pp. 106-135.

[43] *Radio-Québec, pourquoi?* (Montreal: ICEA, 1974); see also, for example, Lise Bouvette, *La télévision communautaire: Analyse sociologique d'une expérience d'animation*, MA thesis (Montreal: Département de sociologie, Université de Montréal, 1973); Jean-François Barbier-Bouvet, Paul Béaud and Patrice Flichy, *Communication et pouvoir: Mass média et média com-*

munautaires au Québec (Paris: Anthropos, 1979); Lesemann and Thiénot, *op. cit.*

[44] Lesemann and Thiénot, *op. cit.*

[45] Lacroix and Lévesque, *loc. cit.* See also Marcel Fournier, "La sociologie québécoise contemporaine", *Recherches sociographiques* 15 (2-3), May-August 1974, pp. 167-199.

[46] Barbier-Bouvet *et al.*, *op. cit.*, pp. 197-198.

[47] France Filiatrault and Gaétan Tremblay, *Inventaire des expériences de média communautaires et populaires au Québec* (Montreal: no publisher indicated, 1976).

[48] "Lettre aux abonnés", *Bulletin* 6, April 21-28, 1971.

[49] *Ibid.*

[50] "L'information et la lutte", an article appended to *Bulletin* 51, March 9-16, 1972.

[51] *Ibid.*

[52] See, for example, *Bulletin* 32, October 21-28, 1971, on censorship at Radio-Canada; and *Bulletin* 34, November 4-11, 1971, on the lock-out at *La Presse*.

[53] See Louis Fournier, "Un réseau d'information alternative: l'Agence de presse libre du Québec", *Le Temps Fou* (13), February-March 1981, pp. 28-33.

[54] "L'APLQ se transforme", *Bulletin* 86, November 16-22, 1972.

[55] *Ibid.*

[56] *Ibid.*

[57] *Bulletin* 92 (Index), December 1972.

[58] For the split within the APLQ and its consequences, see Louis Fournier, *loc. cit.*

[59] See *Ne comptons que sur nos propres moyens* (Montreal: CSN, 1971); *L'État, rouage de notre exploitation* (Montreal: FTQ, 1971); and *L'école au service de la classe dominante* (Quebec City: CEQ, 1971). The importance of the manifesto as a form of political communication is discussed in Gabriel Gagnon and Luc Martin, *Québec 1960-1980: La crise du développement* (Montreal: Hurtubise HMH, 1973), p. 319. Daniel Latouche and Diane Poliquin-Bourassa have anthologized the main political manifestos of the time, with commentary, in *Le manuel de la parole: Manifestes québécois*, Volume 3 (1960-1976), (Montreal: Boréal Express, 1979).

[60] See Michel Pelletier and Yves Vaillancourt, *Du chômage à la libération* (Montreal: Éditions québécoises, 1972).

[61] CSN, *op. cit.*, p. 68.

[62] See Gagnon and Martin, *loc. cit.*

[63] CSN, *op. cit.*

[64] For an overview of the context at the time of the Common Front, see "L'été

chaud des luttes ouvrières", *Bulletin* (APLQ) (18), July 15-22, 1971; and "Dossier: En 71 jours, 23,000 grévistes, 6 grèves sauvages, 17 grèves légales, 6 manifs, 155 arrestations et 1 bombe", *Bulletin* (APLQ) (23), August 19-26, 1971.

[65] See Fernand Daoust, "Le conflit à *La Presse:* les travailleurs québécois politisés grâce au capital", *Point de Mire* 3 (2), October 23, 1971, p. 24.

[66] *Last Post,* "October 1971: Labour comes to the fore", in Auf der Maur and Chodos, *op. cit.,* pp. 91-107.

[67] Case cited in P. Godin, *op. cit.,* p. 262.

[68] Syndicat général des communications, *La Presse* section, "Le dossier noir de l'information à *La Presse*", in *La Grande Tricherie* (Montreal: CSN, 1973).

[69] Quoted in Jean Côté, "Organiser la résistance dans l'information", *Point de Mire* 3 (4), November 6, 1971, pp. 17-20.

[70] *Last Post, loc. cit.*

[71] See P. Fournier, *op. cit.*

[72] "Une lutte à finir contre les exploiteurs", *Point de Mire* 3 (8), December 4, 1971, p. 4.

[73] F. Béliveau, *op. cit.,* p. 138.

[74] See "Des chaudes journées d'automne", *Point de Mire* 3 (8), December 4, 1971, pp. 39-44.

[75] The link between the two Common Fronts, that of *La Presse* and that of the public sector, has been stressed in several analyses made at the time, especially in Piotte, *loc. cit.,* and *Last Post, loc. cit.*

[76] See, for example, Diane Ethier, "L'orientation politique du front commun: L'information et la mobilisation à la base", in Diane Ethier, Jean-Marc Piotte and Jean Reynolds, *Les travailleurs contre l'État bourgeois: avril et mai 1972* (Montreal: Éditions de l'Aurore, 1975), pp. 121-183.

[77] This section is based on Jean-Marc Piotte, "La stratégie du front commun", in Ethier *et al., op. cit.,* pp. 49-118.

[78] This is Diane Ethier's point of view, *loc. cit.*

[79] This section is based on *Last Post,* "Spring 1972: The Strike as Political Weapon", in Auf der Maur and Chodos, *op. cit.,* pp. 109-145; Piotte, *loc. cit.;* articles published in *Québec-Presse,* May 14, 1972; and "Nous contre le gouvernement: sept jours du lutte", *Bulletin* (APLQ) (61), May 18-25, 1972, pp. 1-26.

Chapter 4   Mixed Messages: the 1970s

[1] See Désy *et al., op. cit.*

[2] See CSN, *La Grande tricherie, op. cit.*

[3] See the report on *Québec-Presse* written by the ICEA, *loc. cit.*

[4] See Piotte, *op. cit.* See also Pierre Graveline, *Prenons la parole!* (Montreal: Parti pris, 1978).

[5] *Mobilisation,* second series, (4). This text is also known as "Pour l'organisation politique des travailleurs" ("Towards the Political Organization of the Workers").

[6] See Monière, *op. cit.,* pp. 351-3.

[7] See Penner, *op. cit.*

[8] Désy *et al., op. cit.,* takes a step towards this kind of evaluation.

[9] *Bulletin populaire,* prepublication issue, November 9, 1973.

[10] *Bulletin populaire, loc. cit.*

[11] *Ibid.*

[12] *Bulletin populaire* (8), March 21, 1974.

[13] *Bulletin populaire* (14), June 13, 1974.

[14] *Mobilisation* (2), June 5, 1973.

[15] *Mobilisation* (3), September 1, 1973.

[16] Librairie progressiste, *Liste bibliographique* (Montreal: 1972).

[17] For example, the Centre de recherche et d'information sur le Québec (CRIQ) and the Comité d'information politique (CIP). See *Mobilisation* (3), March 5, 1974.

[18] For a summary attempt to figure out the Quebec far left, see Jacques Benoît, *L'extrême gauche au Québec* (Montreal: La Presse, 1977).

[19] See *Bulletin populaire* (23), November 7, 1974; and *Mobilisation* (4), September 1, 1974.

[20] *Mobilisation* (4), October 2, 1974.

[21] *Mobilisation* (4), December 4, 1974.

[22] *Bulletin populaire* (27), December 19, 1974.

[23] *Bulletin populaire* (32), March 6, 1975.

[24] *Bulletin populaire* (38), May 29, 1975.

[25] "*Mobilisation*: deux années de lutte", *Mobilisation* (4), July 9, 1975.

[26] *Mobilisation* (5), September 1, 1975.

[27] *Liquidons le spontanéisme, l'opportunisme et l'économisme* (Montreal: Mobilisation, 1976).

[28] *Ibid.*

[29] See André Morf, "Les média communautaires au Québec", *Chroniques* (24-25), December 1976-January 1977, pp. 130-145.

[30] See Benoît, *op. cit.*

[31] *Bulletin populaire* (52), January 16, 1976.

[32] *Bulletin populaire* (57), March 25, 1976.

[33] *Bulletin populaire* (58), April 7, 1976.

[34] *Ibid.*

[35] See Désy *et al.*, *op. cit.*

[36] The following is based on Marc Raboy, "Urban Struggles and Municipal Politics: The Montreal Citizens' Movement", *International Review of Community Development* (39-40), 1978, pp. 145-164; and "The Future of Montreal and the M.C.M.", *Our Generation* 12 (4), Fall 1978, pp. 5-18.

[37] "Mais pourquoi donc *Le Jour* est-il disparu en août 1976?", *Le "30"* 1 (9), December 1977, p. 13.

[38] "Le boycottage a-t-il suffi à tuer *Le Jour?*", *Le Devoir*, September 10, 1976.

[39] Pierre Fournier, *op. cit.*

[40] *Le Devoir*, *loc. cit.*; see also Louis Fournier, *loc. cit.*

[41] See Yves Marchaud, "Le putsch des journalistes a précipité la chute du *Jour*", *Le Devoir*, September 10, 1976.

[42] "La Société des rédacteurs du *Jour* a pris en main la rédaction", *Le Jour*, August 24, 1976.

[43] Michaud, *loc. cit.*

[44] Louis Fournier, *loc. cit.*

[45] Jacques Keable, "La grande peur de Radio-Canada", *Québec-Presse*, January 11, 1970.

[46] See Raboy, "La tour infernale . . .", *loc. cit.*

[47] See FPJQ, "Dossier Z", appendix to its *Mémoire*, *op. cit.*

[48] In addition to its important *Mémoire sur la liberté de presse au Québec*, *op. cit.*, the FPJQ published several pertinent reports: for example, *L'information, ça sert à fourrer le monde?*, 1971; *Dossier sur l'information politique au Québec*, 1975; *Historique de la concentration des entreprises de presse au Québec*, 1976. The FNC produced the document *L'information au service des patrons* (Montreal: FNC/CSN, 1975).

[49] See three studies published on the subject in the review *Communication et Information:* Roger De La Garde, "Profil sociodémographique des journalistes de la presse écrite québécoise", 1 (1), August 1975, pp. 31-52; Roger De La Garde and Bernard Barrett, "Profil sociodémographique des journalistes de la presse électronique québécoise", 1 (3), Fall 1976, pp. 259-279; Roger De La Garde and Bernard Barrett, "Profil sociodémographique des journalistes de la presse électronique montréalaise", 2 (2), Fall 1977, pp. 259-280. See also Daniel Marsolais, "Le travailleur de l'information: son rôle", in ICEA, *op. cit.*, pp. 19-20; and Simon Langlois and Florian Sauvageau, "Perception et pratique du journalisme quotidien", *Le Devoir*, January 12, 1982.

[50] See, for example, Lysiane Gagnon, "Journaliste et syndiqué: le perpetuel dilemme", in Florian Sauvageau, Gilles Lesage and Jean De Bonville, eds., *Les Journalistes* (Montreal: Québec-Amérique, 1980), pp. 43-71. See also the FPJQ's magazine *Le "30"* for articles on this subject.

[51] See William Johnson, "Newspapers closed as Quebec reporters wrestle for the reins of power", *Globe and Mail,* October 18, 1977.

[52] Roger Lemelin, "Autopsie de la grève", *La Presse,* May 8, 1978.

[53] *Ibid.*

[54] Several articles published in *Le Devoir* after the 1978 conflicts make useful reading on the subject. For example, Jean-Claude Picard, "Comment l'État doit-il intervenir dans les entreprises de presse?", January 24, 1978; Marcel Pépin, "C'est au public de faire son choix d'un journal et au journaliste de bien pratiquer ce métier exigeant", February 7, 1978; the FPJQ, "Comment l'État peut-il intervenir dans le domaine de l'information?", March 10, 1978; Pierre Godin, "Une année noire pour l'information québécoise", March 23, 1978; Gilles Lesage, "Qui doit contrôler la presse écrite au Québec?", April 22, 1978; Léon Dion, "La crise des médias au Québec", June 23 and 26, 1978; and Florian Sauvageau, "Liberté de presse et droit du public à l'information: fausse opposition ou contradiction véritable?", October 4, 1978.

[55] See Raboy, "La tour infernale . . .", *loc. cit.*

[56] See Jean-Claude Leclerc, "La crise de l'information au *Devoir:* La révolte du 'gars des vues' ", *presse libre* (June 1981).

Chapter 5   Towards Democratic Communications

[1] A.J. Liebling, *The Press* (New York: Pantheon Books, 1975), p. 36.

[2] Armand Mattelart, *Mass Media, Ideologies and the Revolutionary Movement* (Brighton, U.K.: Harvester, 1980/Atlantic Highlands, N.J.: Humanities, 1980).

[3] Angèle Dagenais, "Une soirée en l'honneur de Paul Rose", *Le Devoir,* October 20, 1980.

[4] Quoted in Nathalie Petrowski, "Paul Piché: Conversations dans l'escalier", *Le Devoir,* November 1, 1980.

BIBLIOGRAPHY

I. General works

There exists a vast and growing literature pertinent to the connections between media and social movements. A particularly rich starting point close to the concerns of this study is Hans Magnus Enzensberger's essay "Constituents of a Theory of the Media", first published in English in *New Left Review* and included in the same author's book *The Consciousness Industry* (New York: Seabury Press, 1974).

Two important case studies are Armand Mattelart's *Mass Media, Ideologies and the Revolutionary Movement* (Brighton, U.K.: Harvester, 1980/Atlantic Highlands, N.J.: Humanities, 1980) and Todd Gitlin's *The Whole World is Watching: Mass Media in the Making and Unmaking of the New Left* (Berkeley: UC Press, 1980).

Radical perspectives on communication with a view to social change include the two-volume anthology *Communication and Class Struggle,* Armand Mattelart and Seth Siegelaub, eds. (New York: International General, 1979 and 1983), especially Mattelart's introductions: "For a Class Analysis of Communication" (volume 1) and "For a Class and Group Analysis of Popular Communication Practices" (volume 2). Mattelart is also the co-author, with Michèle Mattelart, of *De l'usage des médias en temps de crise* (Paris: Alain Moreau, 1979).

Important theoretical perspectives on the role of ideology can be found in the writings of British cultural studies scholars such as Stuart Hall and Raymond Williams. There is an overview of work being done in Britain in *Culture, Society and the Media,* M. Gurevitch, T. Bennett, J. Curran and J. Woollacott, eds. (London: Methuen, 1982).

Several American contributions are worth noting: Herbert Schiller's pioneering study of media imperialism *Mass Communications and American Empire* (New York: Augustus Kelley, 1969); James Carey's article "Communication and Culture", *Communication Research* 2 (2), April 1975; and Gaye Tuchman's analysis of the news-framing process, *Making News: A Study in the Construction of Reality* (New York: Free Press, 1978).

The media reform current in the United States is represented in work like Daniel Ben-Horin's "Television Without Tears: An Outline of a Socialist Approach to Popular Television", *Socialist Revolution* 7 (5), September-October 1977, and Douglas Kellner's "TV, Ideology and Emancipatory Popular Culture", *Socialist Review* 9 (3), May-June 1979.

For Canadian contributions, mention must be made of John Porter's "The Ideological System: The Mass Media", in *The Vertical Mosaic* (Toronto: University of Toronto Press, 1965); Dallas W. Smythe, *Dependency Road: Communications, Capitalism, Consciousness, and Canada* (Norwood, N.J.: Ablex Publishing Corp., 1981) and Thelma McCormack, "Revolution, Communication and the Sense of History", in E. Katz and T. Szecsko, eds., *Mass Media and Social Change* (London: Sage, 1981).

II. Quebec social history

In addition to serving as primary source material for our study, the following Quebec periodicals are invaluable general sources for understanding the sixties and seventies in Quebec:

Parti pris (1963-68)
Révolution québécoise (1964-65)
Socialisme and *Socialisme québécois* (1964-69; 1970-74)
Mobilisation (three series: 1969-70; 1971-72; 1973-76)
Point de Mire (1969-72)
Québec-Presse (1969-74)

APLQ *Bulletin* (1971-73)
Bulletin populaire (1973-76)
Le Temps Fou (1978-1983)

And in English:

Our Generation (1961-   )
Last Post (1969-80)

The following works are referred to in the text:

Auf der Maur, Nick, and Chodos, Robert, eds. *Quebec: A Chronicle, 1968-1972* (Toronto: James Lewis and Samuel, 1972).

Benoît, Jacques. *L'extrême gauche au Québec* (Montreal: La Presse, 1977).

Brunelle, Dorval. *La désillusion tranquille* (Montreal: Hurtubise HMH, 1978).

Côté, Charles, and Harnois, Yannik G. *L'animation sociale au Québec: Sources, apports et limites* (Montreal: Éditions coopératives Albert Saint-Martin, 1978).

David, Hélène. "L'état des rapports de classes au Québec de 1945 à 1967", *Sociologie et sociétés* 7 (2) November 1975, pp. 33-66.

Denis, Roch. *Luttes de classe et question nationale au Québec, 1948-1968* (Montreal: Presses socialistes internationales, 1979).

Désy, Marielle; Ferland, Marc; Lévesque, Benoît; and Vaillancourt, Yves. *La conjoncture au Québec au début des années 80: Les enjeux pour le mouvement ouvrier et populaire* (Rimouski: Librairie socialiste de l'est du Québec, 1980).

Ethier, Diane; Piotte, Jean-Marc; and Reynolds, Jean. *Les travailleurs contre l'État bourgeois: avril et mai 1972* (Montreal: Éditions de l'Aurore, 1975).

Fournier, Marcel. "La sociologie québécoise contemporaine", *Recherches sociographiques* 15 (2-3) May-August 1974, pp. 167-199.

Gagnon, Gabriel, and Martin, Luc. *Québec 1960-1980: La crise du développement* (Montreal: Hurtubise HMH, 1973).

Godbout, Jacques, and Collin, Jean-Pierre. *Les organismes populaires en milieu urbain: contre-pouvoir ou nouvelle pratique professionnelle?* (Montreal: INRS-Urbanisation, 1977).

Hamel, Pierre, and Léonard, Jean-François. *Les organizations populaires, l'État et la democratie.* (Montreal: Nouvelle optique, 1981).

Latouche, Daniel, and Poliquin-Bourassa, Diane. *Le Manuel de la parole: Manifestes québécois,* volume 3 (Montreal: Boréal Express, 1979).

Laurendeau, Marc. *Les Québécois violents* (Montreal: Boréal Express, 1974).

Legaré, Anne. "Heures et promesses d'un débat: Les analyses des classes au Québec, 1960-1980", *Les cahiers du socialisme* (5) Spring 1980, pp. 60-84.

Lesemann, Frédéric, and Thiénot, Michel. *Les animations sociales au Québec* (Montreal: Université de Montréal, École de service social, 1972).

McGraw, Donald. *Le développement des groupes populaires à Montréal, 1963-1973* (Montreal: Éditions coopératives Albert Saint-Martin, 1978).

Milner, Sheilagh Hodgins, and Milner, Henry. *The Decolonization of Quebec: An Analysis of Left-Wing Nationalism* (Toronto: McClelland and Stewart, 1973).

Monière, Denis. *Le développement des idéologies au Québec des origines à nos jours* (Montreal: Québec-Amérique, 1977).

Pelletier, Gérard. *La crise d'octobre* (Montreal: Éditions du Jour, 1971).

Pelletier, Michel, and Vaillancourt, Yves. *Du chômage à la libération* (Montreal: Éditions québécoises, 1972).

Penner, Norman. *The Canadian Left: A Critical Analysis* (Scarborough: Prentice-Hall, 1977).

Piotte, Jean-Marc, ed. *Québec-occupé* (Montreal: Parti pris, 1971).

———. *Le syndicalisme de combat* (Montreal: Éditions coopératives Albert Saint-Martin, 1977).

Hamel, Pierre, and Léonard, Jean-François. *Les organisations populaires, l'État et la démocratie* (Montreal: Nouvelle optique, 1981).

Proulx, Serge. "Québec 1945-1980: générations politiques, contre-culture, nouveaux mouvements", in Proulx, Serge, and Vallières, Pierre, eds., *Changer de société* (Montreal: Québec-Amérique, 1982).

Raboy, Marc. "Urban Struggles and Municipal Politics: The Montreal Citizens' Movement", *International Review of Community Development* (39-40) 1978, pp. 145-164.

———. "The Future of Montreal and the MCM", *Our Generation* 12 (4) Fall 1978, pp. 5-18.

Roy, Jean-Louis. *La marche des Québécois: le temps des ruptures, 1945-1960* (Ottawa: Leméac, 1976).

Sansfaçon, Jean-Robert, and Vandelac, Louise. *Perspectives-Jeunesse: Le programme cool d'un gouvernement too much* (Montreal: APLQ, 1972).

Socialisme québécois, "La réaction tranquille". Special issue of *Socialisme québécois* (21-22) April 1971.

Vallières, Pierre. "Introduction", *La Liberté en friche* (Montreal: Québec-Amérique, 1979).

III. The Quebec media

a) Books and journal articles

Barbier-Bouvet, Jean-François; Béaud, Paul; and Flichy, Patrice. *Communication et pouvoir: Mass média et média communautaires au Québec* (Paris: Anthropos, 1979).

Beauchamp, Michel. *Initiatives militantes et communications* (Quebec City: CEQ, 1974).

Béliveau, François. *Pogné* (Montreal: Éditions québécoises, 1971).

Benjamin, Jacques. "Pouvoir politique et médias au Québec", *Communication et Information* 3 (1) 1979, pp. 67-77.

Bouvette, Lise. *La télévision communautaire: Analyse sociologique d'une expérience d'animation*, MA thesis (Montreal: Département de sociologie, Université de Montréal, 1973).

B.R., journaliste. "Une information 'totalitaire', prise à son propre piège", in Jean-Marc Piotte, ed., *Québec-occupé* (Montreal: Parti pris, 1971), pp. 179-216.

———. "L'information au Québec: de la politique à la consommation", *Socialisme québécois* (21-22) April 1971, pp. 79-108.

Caron, Normand. "Mais où est donc passé *Québec-Presse*?", *Dossiers 'Vie ouvrière'* 28 (125) May 1978, pp. 288-91.

Clement, Wallace. "The Media Elite: Gatekeepers of Ideas", and "Structure and Concentration of Canada's Mass Media", chapters 7 and 8 in *The Canadian Corporate Elite: An Analysis of Economic Power* (Toronto: McClelland and Stewart, 1975), pp. 270-286 and 287-324.

Commission parlementaire spéciale sur les problèmes de la liberté de presse. *Rapport préliminaire: Les travaux de la commission en 1969* (Quebec City: Assemblée nationale du Québec, 1972).

Côté, Jean. "Organiser la résistance dans l'information", *Point de Mire* 3 (4) November 6, 1971, pp. 17-20.

―――. *La communication au Québec* (Repentigny: Éditions Point de Mire, 1974).

Daignault, Richard. "Les syndicats et l'information du public", in *Le public et l'information en relations de travail* (Quebec City: Les presses de l'Université Laval, Département des relations industrielles, 1969), pp. 99-116.

Daoust, Fernand. "Le conflit à *La Presse*: les travailleurs québécois politisés grâce au capital", *Point de Mire* 3 (2) October 23, 1971, p. 24.

De La Garde, Roger. "Profil sociodémographique des journalistes de la presse écrite québécoise", *Communication et Information* 1 (1) August 1975, pp. 31-52.

―――, and Barrett, Bernard. "Profil sociodémographique des journalistes de la presse électronique québécoise", *Communication et Information* 1 (3) Fall 1976, pp. 259-279.

―――, and ―――. "Profil sociodémographique des journalistes de la presse électronique montréalaise", *Communication et Information* 2 (2) Fall 1977, pp. 259-280.

Dossiers 'Vie ouvrière'. "Le pouvoir de l'information" (1) and (2). Two special issues of *Dossiers 'Vie ouvrière'* 28 (125 and 126) May 1978 and June-July 1978.

Filiatraul, France, and Tremblay, Gaétan. *Inventaire des expériences de médias communautaires et populaires au Québec* (Montreal: no publisher indicated, 1976).

Financial Post. "Inside the Media", special report, September 22, 1979.

Fortin, Gérald. "Notes de recherches: Les changements d'attitudes et de personnalité produits par l'animation sociale et les mass médias", *Recherches sociographiques* 9 (3) September-December 1968, pp. 310-312.

Fournier, Louis. "Mais pourquoi donc *Le Jour* est-il disparu en août 1976?", *Le "30"* 1 (9) December 1977, p. 13.

―――. "Une expérience de presse engagée: *Québec-Presse* il y a dix ans", *Le "30"* 3 (3) March 1979, p. 22.

―――. "Un réseau d'information alternative: l'Agence de presse libre du Québec", *Le Temps Fou* (13) February-March 1981, pp. 28-33.

Fournier, Pierre. "Institutional Penetration: The Case of the Media", chapter 6 of *The Quebec Establishment* (Montreal: Black Rose Books, 1976), pp. 98-108.

Godin, Pierre. *L'information-opium: Une histoire politique du journal "La Presse"* (Montreal: Parti pris, 1972).

Graveline, Pierre. *Prenons la parole!* (Montreal: Parti pris, 1978).

Hamelin, Jean, and Beaulieu, André. "Aperçu du journalisme québécois d'expression française", *Recherches sociographiques* 7 (3) September-December 1966, pp. 305-348.

ICEA. *La parole ça se prend* (Montreal: CEQ/ICEA, 1980).

——. "*Québec-Presse* 1969-1974: Le bilan de l'ICEA", in *Québec-Presse*, May 1, 1981, published as a special issue of the bulletin of the ICEA 4 (5) May 1981.

Lacroix, Jean-Guy, and Lévesque, Benoît. "L'unification et la fragmentation des appareils idéologiques au Canada et au Québec: le cas de la radio-télévision", *Les cahiers du socialisme* (5) Spring 1980, pp. 106-135.

Latouche, Daniel. "Mass Media and Communication in a Canadian Political Crisis", in Benjamin Singer, ed., *Communications in Canadian Society* (Toronto: Copp Clark, 1975), pp. 374-385.

Lévesque, Benoît. "Les communications et le développement", *Possibles* 2 (2/3) Winter-Spring 1978, pp. 79-96.

——. "Sens politique de l'animation sociale et des communications dans les organismes communautaires et coopératives", in Benoît Lévesque, ed., *Animation sociale, entreprises communautaires et coopératives* (Montreal: Éditions coopératives Albert Saint-Martin, 1979), pp. 318-334.

Maintenant. "Les véritables maîtres du Québec", dossier in *Maintenant* (86) May 1969, pp. 144-155.

Maistre, Gilbert. "Aperçu socio-économique de la presse quotidienne québécoise", *Recherches sociographiques* 12 (1) January-April 1971, pp. 105-115.

Major, Robert. *Parti pris: Idéologies et littérature* (Montreal: Hurtubise HMH, 1979).

Matthieu, Gilles. "Le journalisme et la lutte des classes", *Révolution québécoise* 1 (2) October 1964, pp. 28-34.

Moore, Marie-France. "*Mainmise,* version québécoise de la contre-culture", *Recherches sociographiques* 14 (3) 1973, pp. 363-381.

Morf, André. "Les médias communautaires au Québec", *Chroniques* (24-25) December 1976-January 1977, pp. 130-145.

Multi-Réso. *La presse écrite au Québec: Bilan et prospective* (Quebec City: Ministry of Communications, 1977).

Pelletier, Gérard. "The Strike and the Press", in Pierre Elliott Trudeau, ed., *The Asbestos Strike* (Toronto: James Lorimer and Company, 1974).

Point de Mire. "Une lutte à finir contre les exploiteurs", *Point de Mire* 3 (8) December 4, 1974, p. 4.

———. "Des chaudes journées d'automne", *Point de Mire* 3 (8) December 4, 1971, pp. 39-44.

Raboy, Marc. "La tour infernale: la petite histoire de l'information à Radio-Canada", *Le Temps Fou* (14) April-May 1981, pp. 18-22.

Recherches sociographiques. Special issue on the mass media, *Recherches sociographiques* 12 (1) January 1971.

Reid, Malcolm. *The Shouting Signpainters: A Literary and Political Account of Quebec Revolutionary Nationalism* (Toronto: McClelland and Stewart, 1972).

Revue internationale d'action communautaire. "Média communautaires ou média libres". Special issue, 6 (46) Fall 1981.

Rochefort, Jean. "La vérité sur *La Presse*", *Révolution québécoise* 1 (3) November 1964, pp. 6-11.

Roy, Michel. "La grève des réalisateurs de Radio-Canada", *Relations industrielles* 14 (2) April 1959, pp. 265-276.

Royal Commission on Newspapers. (Ottawa: Minister of Supply and Services Canada, 1981).

Sauvageau, Florian; Lesage, Gilles; and De Bonville, Jean, eds. *Les journalistes* (Montreal: Québec-Amérique, 1980).

Siegel, Arthur. *Canadian Newspaper Coverage of the FLQ Crisis: A Study of the Impact of the Press on Politics,* PhD thesis (Montreal: Department of Political Science, McGill University, 1974).

Socialisme 69. "Dossier: Information et enfermement culturel", *Socialisme 69* (17) April-May-June 1969, pp. 58-128.

SORECOM. *Enquête sur la diffusion de l'information au Québec* (Quebec City: Commission parlementaire spéciale sur les problèmes de la liberté de presse, Assemblée nationale du Québec, 1972).

Special Senate Committee on Mass Media. *Mass Media* (Ottawa: Queen's Printer, 1970).

Versailles, André. *Communications*, a bibliography (Montreal: Conseil de développement social du Montréal Métropolitain, 1972).

b) Newspaper articles

Dagenais, Angèle. "Une soirée en honneur de Paul Rose", *Le Devoir*, October 20, 1980.

Denis, Roch. "*Québec-Presse* doit se brancher", *Québec-Presse*, October 27, 1974.

Dion, Léon. "La crise des médias au Québec", *Le Devoir*, June 23 and June 26, 1978.

FPJQ. "Comment l'État peut-il intervenir dans le domaine de l'information?", *Le Devoir*, March 10, 1978.

Godin, Gérald. "Les amis de *Québec-Presse* et la censure", *Québec-Presse*, October 22, 1972.

Godin, Pierre. "Une année noire pour l'information québécoise", *Le Devoir*, March 23, 1978.

Gruman, Barry. "Good reading for shareholders", *Financial Post* supplement, November 19, 1977.

Johnson, William. "Newspapers closed as Quebec reporters wrestle for the reins of power", *Globe and Mail*, October 18, 1977.

Keable, Jacques. "La grande peur de Radio-Canada", *Québec-Presse*, January 11, 1970.

Langlois, Simon, and Sauvageau, Florian. "Perception et pratique du journalisme quotidien", *Le Devoir*, January 12, 1982.

Leclerc, Jean-Claude. "La crise de l'information au *Devoir:* la révolte du 'Gars des vues' ", *presse libre*, June 1981.

Le Devoir. "Le boycottage a-t-il suffi à tuer *Le Jour?*", *Le Devoir*, September 10, 1976.

———. "Profits records pour le canal 10", *Le Devoir*, July 13, 1978.

Le Jour. "La Société des rédacteurs du *Jour* a pris en main la rédaction", *Le Jour*, August 24, 1976.

Lemelin, Roger. "Autopsie de la grève", *La Presse*, May 8, 1978.

Lesage, Gilles. "Qui doit contrôler la presse écrite au Québec?", *Le Devoir*, April 22, 1978.

Michaud, Yves. "Le putsch des journalistes a précipité la chute du *Jour*", *Le Devoir*, September 10, 1976.

Nadeau, Michel. "Civitas s'attaque au marché anglophone pour préparer une expansion nord-américaine", *Le Devoir*, November 12, 1980.

———. "Les journaux québécois de Péladeau ont réalisé $12 millions de profits", *Le Devoir*, January 22, 1981.

Pépin, Marcel. "C'est au public de faire son choix d'un journal et au journaliste de bien pratiquer ce métier exigeant", *Le Devoir,* February 7, 1978.

Petrowski, Nathalie. "Paul Piché: Conversations dans l'escalier", *Le Devoir,* November 1, 1980.

Picard, Jean-Claude. "Comment l'État peut-il intervenir dans le domaine de l'information?", *Le Devoir,* March 10, 1978.

Sauvageau, Florian. "Liberté de presse et droit du public à l'information: Fausse opposition ou contradiction véritable?", *Le Devoir,* October 4, 1978.

IV. Documents

APLQ. "L'information et la lutte", appended to *Bulletin* 51, March 9-16, 1972.

CEQ. *L'école au service de la classe dominante* (Quebec City: CEQ, 1971).

CFP. *Les militants et les médias d'information* (Montreal: CFP, 1978).

CSN. *Le Deuxième Front* (Montreal: CSN, 1968).

———. *Ne comptons que sur nos propres moyens* (Montreal: CSN, 1971).

———. *La Grande Tricherie* (Montreal: CSN, 1973).

———. *Boycottons Radiomutuel* (Montreal: CSN, 1977).

FNC. *L'information au service des patrons* (Montreal: FNC/CSN, 1975).

FPJQ. *L'information, ça sert à fourrer le monde?* (Montreal: FPJQ, 1971).

———. *Mémoire sur la liberté de presse au Québec* (Montreal: FPJQ, 1972).

———. *Dossier sur l'information politique au Québec* (Montreal: FPJQ, 1975).

———. *Historique de la concentration des entreprises de presse au Québec* (Montreal: FPJQ, 1976).

———. *Conséquences et remèdes à la concentration des entreprises de presse au Québec* (Montreal: FPJQ, 1976).

Front commun sur les communications. *Dossier noir sur la radio et la télévision commerciales* (Montreal: ICEA, 1977).

FTQ. *L'État, rouage de notre exploitation* (Montreal: FTQ, 1971).

Gagnon, Charles. *Pour le parti prolétarien* (Montreal: L'Équipe du journal, 1972).

ICEA. *Radio-Québec pourquoi?* (Montreal: ICEA, 1974).

————. *Ça saute aux yeux: Il faut démocratiser Radio-Québec* (Montreal: ICEA, 1974).

————. *Consultation publique sur l'orientation de Radio-Québec* (Montreal: ICEA, 1976).

————. *La concentration et le contrôle de l'information* (Montreal: ICEA, 1980).

Mobilisation. Pour l'organisation politique des travailleurs (Montreal: *Mobilisation*, 1972).

————. *Liquidons le spontanéisme, l'opportunisme et l'économisme* (Montreal: *Mobilisation*, 1976).

Parti pris. "L'information, une arme idéologique", *Parti pris* 2 (2) October 1964, pp. 2-4.